W9-AXY-985

Teach Your Child Nighttime Control—Overnight!

- Forming a bedwetting agreement
- Training your child to hold back
- Understanding that "full feeling"
- Teaching your child to change the bed sheets
- Helping your child to increase bladder capacity
- How to effectively use the pad-and-buzzer method
- Coping with temper tantrums and refusal to practice
- Creating a dry-bed calendar progress chart
- Getting the whole family to help
- When and how to give rewards

A Parent's Guide to Bedwetting Control
A Step-by-Step Method

Nathan H. Azrin, Ph.D.
Victoria A. Besalel, Ph.D.

PUBLISHED BY POCKET BOOKS NEW YORK

POCKET BOOKS, a Simon & Schuster division of
GULF & WESTERN CORPORATION
1230 Avenue of the Americas, New York, N.Y. 10020

Published by arrangement with Simon and Schuster
Library of Congress Catalog Card Number: 79-17008

ISBN: 0-671-82774-X

First Pocket Books printing June, 1981

10 9 8 7 6 5 4 3 2 1

POCKET and colophon are trademarks of Simon & Schuster.

Printed in the U.S.A.

Contents

Foreword

Why write a book about bedwetting? Doesn't everyone simply outgrow the problem? These are the same questions asked when the earlier book *Toilet Training in Less Than a Day* was written. Both books seemed to be dealing with a problem that didn't exist except for a very few children. But the reaction of parents to the earlier book on toilet training was substantial and indicated that the toilet-training problem was of great concern to parents, perhaps to most parents.

So, too, does bedwetting seem to be a problem of universal concern, but which is generally considered a rarity because it is seldom discussed and only in extreme cases to be considered serious enough to seek out professional assistance. Bedwetting is a "closet problem," by its very nature concealed from the awareness of all but members of the immediate family. Yet, survey studies reveal that millions of children have the bedwetting problem long after the age at which popular opinion considers it to be absent and often persisting into the teenage years. Consequently, this book has been written in the hope that it will help parents learn how to deal with the bedwetting problem, rather than to hope in vain that the child will suddenly outgrow it.

This book is a self-help book intended to provide information whereby the parents can do something about eliminating the bedwetting problem. The principal reason for eliminating bedwetting is, of course, the many benefits to the child, rather than just for the convenience of the parent. In this spirit of emphasizing the child's perspective, the training program is designed to involve the child as a partner in the program, rather than as the unwilling object of a training program imposed on him. Accordingly, the training program is a self-help program for the child, as well as of the parents. The child is given a thorough explanation of the rationale of the program. If the child is very young, his understanding is enhanced by a bedtime story (Chapter 10) describing the efforts of a fictitious bedwetter with whom he can identify. For the older child, we recommend that he read this book along with his parents. The self-help is intended to be a joint effort.

How likely is it that the parents and child will receive help from the program described in this self-help book? We hope that many, and even most, readers will be successful, but recognize that no training method for any problem is successful with everyone. Bedwetting is no exception, and even for those children for whom the training program is effective, individual differences always exist, with some children requiring a longer period than others. To provide the reader with informed expectations regarding the likelihood of success, we have taken pains to summarize the results obtained in the published studies using the present program. Similarly, we have taken care to describe the results of those studies in terms of the percentage reduction of bedwetting, rather than merely as cured or not cured, and to provide information about the duration of the benefit. The benefits were substantial, but no miracle should be expected, and some children may require considerably more time and effort than the "average child." And, unfortunately, some children may, of course, not benefit from the program depending in part on how well the training is done, but also in part because of the inevitable individual differences between children.

Although success cannot be guaranteed for any training program for any problem, as we have noted, considerable research has been carried out with the present program before writing this self-help book. This research has covered several years during which the procedures have been tested in several published studies with children and parents of very different backgrounds and age levels.

To simplify and improve the training program, changes have been made continually as problems have emerged. Controlled comparisons have been made in the studies with alternative methods of treating bedwetting in order to discover how much more effective the new program is. Professional trainers have been used in some of the studies to assure that the training program was being followed as intended. In other studies, the parent did all of the training after being instructed by the trainer. And, finally, we have tested the success of parents who, after reading about this program, trained their children with little or no outside assistance. All of these studies have attempted to develop a training method that would be effective for the largest percentage of children in the shortest time and with minimal inconvenience. The favorable results obtained in the studies showed that, even though no overnight cure of bedwetting could be guaranteed for all children, the training program was substantially effective with most of the children in a fairly short time when the training was performed correctly.

A noteworthy feature of this instructional method is that we tested its effectiveness by giving a copy of the procedures to several parents to learn how to train their children. Changes in the writing were made to correct passages that were reported as unclear. The preliminary results are that bedwetting stopped for about two-thirds of the children and was greatly reduced for the other third. These results indicate that this book can serve as the means of stopping bedwetting for most children, but that professional assistance may still be required for some.

Is the present method the final answer to the bedwetting problem? Definitely not. Research is actively being conducted by many investigators on new methods, and better ones should be available as their results become known. Meanwhile, the authors also will continue their studies on how to improve the treatment for bedwetting and, when sufficient progress is made, to revise and update this book. In this manner we hope to give parents a better understanding of the bedwetting problem and information on new training methods to alleviate it.

Gender-specific pronouns present a problem in referring to the child who is to be trained. To avoid the awkwardness of the he/she or him/her designations, the authors have used the male designations "he" and "him" —in large part because the majority of bedwetters are male. We hope that appropriate pronouns will emerge which are not gender-specific and this problem will not exist in the future.

The assistance of many individuals is sincerely acknowledged.

Robert S. Buffington drew the preliminary sketches on which the illustrations in this book were based.

Much of the writing of this book occurred while the senior author was a Fellow at the Center for Advanced Study in the Behavioral Sciences in Stanford, California.

Many individuals assisted and participated in the development and testing of the new training program over a period of many years; these include T. Sneed, L. Denno, R. Foxx, D. Millard, and P. Thienes.

Much of the writing of this book occurred while the senior author was a Fellow at the Center for Advanced Study in the Behavioral Sciences in Stanford, California.

1 How Much of a Problem Is Bedwetting?

How Common Is Bedwetting?

Bedwetting is a very common problem; just how common depends on the age of the child. During the first year of life, all children wet their bed and we accept this as a normal development. So, in a sense, bedwetting is universal. However, when the child learns to toilet himself during the day at the age of two or three years, we feel that he has developed control over his bladder and should be able to stay dry at night. Most children do, in fact, stop wetting their beds by the age of three or four years. Yet, many children do not. Many studies have been done to determine when children stop wetting their bed. The results are surprising in revealing just how many children continue bedwetting long after they have learned to stay dry during the day.

For children three years of age, over one-third are wetting their bed.

For the four-year-old, the percentage of bedwetters has decreased greatly to about one out of four, still a large fraction.

For the five- and six-year-old children, who are just enrolling in school for the first time, about one in seven are still wetting their bed. Two or three years have passed since the children had achieved bladder control during the day. Yet, in a school class of thirty children, about three or four are still having a problem.

At eight or nine years of age, long after infancy, one in about every fifteen children is still bedwetting, which means two children in an average-sized class of fourth and fifth graders.

As adolescence approaches at the ages of twelve to fourteen, one would expect that bedwetting would be a dim memory of the process of growing up. But still, about one in every twenty-five children has not "outgrown" the problem.

And at full maturity, seventeen or eighteen years of age, one in every fifty persons still has the problem. Studies of army draftees have discovered that about 2 percent of the soldiers wet their bed at night.

Some of the studies and books that have revealed these statistics are listed in the References section at the back of the book. References are also given to the other facts about bedwetting to be described later for the reader who desires to read more about this topic or to read the original reports. The general pattern that emerges from the studies on bedwetting at different ages is that it does not suddenly disappear for all children at the age of two years, or three years, or four years. Rather, a progressive but gradual decrease occurs between infancy and adulthood in the proportion of persons who have the problem.

About twice as many boys are bedwetters as girls.

Boys versus Girls

Girls do not wet their bed as often as boys do. Bedwetting is about twice as common among boys as among girls. This difference is true at each age level. There is no explanation for this difference, although the reason may be physical. Another possibility is that boys are often treated differently than girls and parents may be less insistent with them about bedwetting as with so many other problems. Yet, in every country for which surveys have been published, boys are at least 50 percent more likely to be wetting their bed and usually twice as likely.

15

Bedwetting Is a Secret

Because bedwetting is commonly considered to be a problem of infancy, it is usually kept secret when it persists after infancy. Children are ashamed to let other children know. Parents often take pride when their child stops bedwetting at an early age and will conceal the problem if their child continues. Other types of growing-up problems such as thumb-sucking or wetting one's pants during the day are highly visible. Everyone can tell whether a child wears diapers during the day, or wets his pants, or sucks his thumb. But bedwetting occurs at night and no one need know except the child and the parent. Consequently, bedwetting is a private problem and for that reason is undoubtedly much more common than the survey results indicate, since parent and child alike are often embarrassed to admit it.

The truest information about bedwetting should come from studies which actually count the number of wet beds. But such studies are possible only in institutions such as hospitals, orphanages, institutions for problem children, training institutions for retarded children, summer camps, and other places where large numbers of children sleep overnight. Indeed, observations of this direct nature have been made in a few instances and reveal that bedwetting is far more extensive than the embarrassed questionnaire reports indicated. Direct observations of young children in an Israeli kibbutz reported by M. Kaffman in 1972 revealed that up to five years of age about 30 percent of the children were still bedwetting. In another set of direct observations in 1970 in an institution of 321 deaf children, five to nineteen years of age, Baller and Giangreco found that over 40 percent of the children were wetting their bed every night. In a classic study by the Mowrers in 1938, half of the twenty-four children, four to twelve years of age, in their Children's Community Center in New Haven, Connecticut, were bedwetters. If one were to judge from the questionnaire reports, bedwetting should be absent among fully mature adults. Yet, as was mentioned previously, about one out of every fifty military recruits was found to be bedwetting. Because it is so embarrassing to admit bedwetting, the myth exists that very few children have the problem when in fact it is very common. If your child is wetting the bed, whatever the child's age, you can be assured that many, many children of the same age also have the problem. And possibly, just as you and your children may have done, they and their parents are keeping it a secret.

How Many Persons Are Bedwetters?

Let us consider that bedwetting is a normal part of growing up during the first two years and that it is only a problem when a child is three years old or older. How many persons are bedwetting after three years of age? We have made a calculation based on the number of children at each age level as revealed by the Census Bureau reports, and by the results of the studies for each age group. The answer is about five million persons in the United States. This estimate, based on the questionnaire reports which we saw, may be an understatement. The true number may be closer to ten million persons who are bedwetters.

What Inconveniences Are Caused by Bedwetting?

Since bedwetting occurs in the dark of night, one might conclude that no inconvenience would result. But, the reactions of parents and children demonstrate that the problem is very real. The various reasons for wishing to solve the bedwetting problem are probably best stated by listing typical statements made by the parents of these children.

HIS BROTHERS TEASE

My boy is eight years old and has never had a dry night. His two brothers, who are five and seven years old, are never wet and whenever they have a quarrel they call him "pee-baby" and tease him so much that he doesn't want to play with them.

IT SMELLS

If I don't do anything about it, her room smells like a toilet in some of the train stations I've been in. So, I change her sheets as quickly as I can each day and spray the room with a sweet-smelling fragrance to hide the smell.

NO CAMP

He is dying to go to camp each summer. All of his friends are away then. But he is too scared to go because of what will happen when he wets his bed there. I don't blame him.

SHE HATES HER CRIB

I know I should get her a regular bed and not keep her in the crib. She's seven years old. But I don't want to spend a lot of money on a good bed that she is going to dirty up every night. I'll wait until she stops.

CAN'T SPEND OVERNIGHT WITH FRIENDS

His friends are always inviting each other for sleep-overs at each other's house, especially on weekends and vacations. Whenever he is invited he makes up excuses. And, of course, he'd never dare to invite anybody else over to sleep with him.

HE WON'T OUTGROW IT—FOURTEEN YEARS OLD

Every year since he was four years old I think that he'll outgrow it soon, and I needn't worry. But here he is looking like a grown-up man and still the same.

NO LONG TRIPS OR VISITING

My husband and I try to keep regular contact with our parents who live a day's drive away. Sarah wet the bed in my parents' house the last time we visited when Sarah was five years old. Since then we haven't taken Sarah after all the apologies I had to make. We just don't go on long trips very often anymore. She's too young to leave behind.

NO SLEEPING BAGS

He's twelve years old and wants a sleeping bag just like his friends to go camping with them. But how would you dry out a soggy sleeping bag? And how could he hide it from his friends?

THAT RUBBER SHEET

The last time my daughter had her girlfriend over to the house, the girlfriend sat on the bed and felt the rubber sheet crinkling under her. My daughter was so ashamed that now she won't invite any friends over.

CHANGING BED SHEETS

I change the bed sheets once a week for all of the beds except Julie's. For eleven years now, I have had to change her sheets and make up her bed and wash her pajamas every single day. Thank God for washing machines and dryers. But, what a waste of money, and all that trouble every day.

NO DRINKS FOR DEBBIE

It's an unwritten rule around our house now. No soda or milk or drinks or ice cream for Debbie after supper or before bedtime. At first she objected, but now she'll refuse even when a friend offers it to her.

I CAN'T HELP IT, MOMMY

I was told not to punish my child for bedwetting and that she would outgrow it if I just ignored the problem and didn't make her upset about it. My disappointment must show through though, because whenever she sees me check the bed, or change the sheets, she tells me it's not her fault.

Children who bed-wet are ashamed to go to camp.

SPANKINGS DIDN'T HELP

My mother said she handled the problem with all her children by spanking them and taking away privileges. I didn't like the idea but after six years I tried it in desperation. My son became so terrified of me, I stopped after two months and decided to live with it.

The seriousness of the problem of bedwetting goes far beyond the distress of embarrassment or inconvenience for the child. The annoyance to the parent can reach the point where the parent vents his or her frustration with harsh punishment of the child. Since bedwetting is so serious a problem for the child, we can understand why so much attention has been directed to discovering a cure both by parents as well as by professional persons, including the present authors. In the following chapter, we shall examine the effectiveness of some of these proposed remedies, including medical, psychological, and family remedies, with special attention to a newly developed educational method. We shall see that some methods of effective treatment are now available and that the bedwetting children and their parents no longer must suffer the consequences of this problem without hope.

2 | Methods of Treating Bedwetting— Common Practice and Professional Treatments

*What Are the Chances That My Child
Will Outgrow It?*

Many different types of treatment are currently being used to treat bedwetting, the simplest method being to do nothing more than common practice. We can ask what the chances will be that our child will stop bedwetting within the next year if we do nothing more than common practice. The answer to this question has been provided by examining the results of the surveys which showed how common bedwetting is at different ages.

If your child is three or four years old, there is a 25 percent chance that bedwetting will stop during the next year.

If your child is five to nine years old, there is only a 20 percent chance that he will stop bedwetting during the next year.

If your child is ten to fourteen years old, the chances are only 15 percent that bedwetting will stop during the next year.

These calculations can be stated differently.

If your child is bedwetting at three or four years of age, the chances are 75 percent that bedwetting will still be a problem a year from now.

And if your child is bedwetting at thirteen or fourteen years of age, the chances are 85 percent that a year from now his bedwetting will still be with you.

What if you wait longer than a year? What are the chances of a spontaneous cure during the next two years? or three years? five years? ten years?

If your child is bedwetting at six years of age, the chances are 66 percent that he will still be bedwetting two years from now, 54 percent that he'll be bedwetting three years from now, and 37 percent that he'll still be bedwetting five years from now. Even ten years from now there is a 16 percent chance that the sixteen-year-old child will still be wetting his bed.

Children will eventually outgrow bedwetting under common and ordinary practices, but the chances of that happening soon are not very high.

What Are Some of the Common Methods of Treating Bedwetting?

We have just seen that the chances of stopping bedwetting within one year are less than 25 percent under common family practices. What are these commonly used practices which have been so ineffective?

The most common procedure seems to be to restrict the fluid intake. The child is not allowed to have any drinks before bedtime in the reasonable expectation that if there is less fluid in the bladder, the child will be less likely to urinate at night.

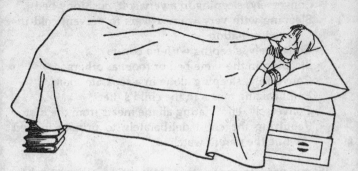

Unusual remedies have been used for bedwetting, including raising the level of the foot of the bed.

Another common procedure is to awaken the child regularly throughout the night and to require the child to toilet at those times. Parents often attempt a schedule of toileting their child every two hours or even every hour, but usually abandon the effort after one or two nights because of the sleeplessness that results for them as well as the child.

Punishment is used by many parents, especially as other efforts fail. Punishment takes the form of scolding, spanking, belittling comparisons, and shaming. The child himself usually feels that he is being punished for an action over which he has no control.

Some of the less common family treatments are:

> Requiring the child to sleep only on his back
> Conversely, requiring the child to sleep on his stomach
> Raising the head of the bed
> Conversely, raising the foot of the bed
> Sleeping on a very hard surface or on the floor

Conversely, sleeping in a very soft, cushiony bed
Sleeping with very warm covers to prevent cold-induced urination
Conversely, sleeping with no covers
Sleeping in the same bed or room as others
Conversely, sleeping alone in a separate room
Emphasizing meats in the child's diet
Conversely, eliminating all the meats from the diet
Requiring the child deliberately to urinate in bed while the parent watched

Some parents report that bedwetting stopped when they used one of the methods described above, but the chances are that coincidence was responsible for their belief. The situation is somewhat similar to having a common cold. Bedwetting, like the common cold, eventually disappears for almost everyone even if one does nothing for it. If the bedwetting, or the cold, happens to stop after a new treatment was started for a child, the parents understandably, but mistakenly, conclude that the treatment cured the bedwetting or the cold. No scientific tests of the above family remedies have been conducted, so we cannot say that any of them have been proved to be valueless. We can say, however, that as a group these family remedies seem to have little value since we saw that bedwetting shows only a slight decrease from year to year even though one or another of these remedies has been used by almost all parents of children who wet their beds.

Indeed, several of the home remedies prescribe the opposite of other home remedies, such as sleeping with covers versus sleeping with no covers, or sleeping alone versus sleeping with others. Similarly, we have seen that some parents believe in punishment for bedwetting as a remedy, whereas another school of thought believes that punishment perpetuates the problem. The most common home remedy is to restrict fluids, but in this case experimental evidence exists demonstrating that an increase of fluids is beneficial because of the resulting increased ability of the bladder to retain urine. We must conclude that experimental evidence is needed before we can trust any home remedy, however reasonable that remedy may seem.

Professional Treatments

The bedwetting problem has not been ignored by professional persons and scientists. As early as the sixteenth century, the medical profession had recognized it as a problem and various treatments were considered, especially medicines and special diets. Scientific tests of treatments have occurred only very recently, however. We will describe briefly the four major types of treatment now being used by the medical and psychological professions.

MEDICAL TREATMENT OF BEDWETTING

What percentage of bedwetting cases are caused by a medical problem? Medical examination of bedwetters has shown that about 1 or 2 percent of the children who wet their bed have medical problems that could account for the bedwetting. If a medical cause is suspected, then there should be a medical examination and treatment before attempting special training procedures. For almost all (98 percent) bedwetting children, however, no specific medical cause of the problem is likely to be discovered.

PSYCHOTHERAPY AS A TREATMENT FOR BEDWETTING

A common belief is that emotional problems and nervousness cause bedwetting. Psychotherapy is occasionally used for this reason to resolve existing emotional problems in the hope that the bedwetting will then stop. Unfortunately, the studies that have used psychotherapy for this purpose have not provided encouraging results. The psychotherapy usually extends over a period of many months and only a small percentage of the children are cured of bedwetting during that time. If a child has emotional problems, treatment should certainly be considered for those problems in their own right, but little help for bedwetting should be expected.

DRUG TREATMENT OF BEDWETTING

One drug, imipramine, has recently come into wide usage as a method of controlling bedwetting, and several studies have been conducted of its effectiveness. The evidence is clear that this drug does produce some benefit. The drug is taken each day by the child and is effective in stopping bedwetting for about half of the children, but only as long as the drug is taken. Of those children who stop taking it, only about 30 percent of them are cured, which is not much different, as we have seen, from the results obtained when no drug was used and one simply waited for the child to outgrow the problem. The drug has several undesirable side effects, especially at the higher doses at which the drug has more effect. Some medical authorities have criticized the use of this drug by children for periods of months and years since the child becomes dependent on its use as a substitute for learning nighttime bladder control. Nevertheless, the drug does have a fairly immediate effect and can be of great usefulness as a short-term relief for bedwetting for some children.

URINE-SIGNAL METHOD

The fourth current method of treating bedwetting is to provide an automatic signal to the child at the moment that he starts wetting his bed. The method is often called the pad-and-buzzer procedure, since a moisture-sensitive pad is placed under the bed sheet and a buzzer sounds when the pad becomes moistened by urine. The pad is put in place before the child goes to bed and the buzzer, which can be placed nearby on a dresser, will sound within a few seconds after wetting starts at any time during the night. When the child is awakened by the buzzer, he arises from bed to complete the urination in the toilet. The bed is remade with dry sheets, the alarm is reset, and the pad is replaced so that any additional wettings that night will again provide an awakening signal. Several companies manufacture this urine-signaling apparatus and it is available from some large mail-order companies at a cost of $25 to $50.

Many studies have tested the pad-and-buzzer method. The signaling procedure has been effective for about 90 percent of the children. The average child requires about two months of use of the apparatus. For about one-fourth of the children who were successful, bedwetting started again some time after the apparatus was discontinued. But, if the apparatus was used again, the bedwetting again stopped.

These results with the pad and buzzer are impressive indeed compared to the results obtained by the other forms of treatment. In fact, direct comparison tests have been made and show that the pad-and-buzzer method is far superior to either psychotherapy or to the drugs.

But, the pad-and-buzzer method is not without its

problems. Surveys show that about one-half of the parents say that they would rather not use the pad-and-buzzer method. Some of the problems mentioned are:

The parent must awaken in the middle of the night to reset the apparatus and change the bed, often twice a night, for several weeks.

The treatment is not usually effective immediately but rather requires several weeks for the average child, and months for some.

The buzzer may awaken other children in the house.

The buzzer may interrupt the parents at night at moments when they especially desire privacy.

The child may deliberately disconnect the apparatus before going to sleep.

The child's perspiration in hot weather sometimes causes the alarm to sound in the middle of the night even though the child had not urinated.

The apparatus can become defective through use or abuse and fail to sound even though the child has wet.

The cost of the apparatus and the replacement sensing pads is more than some parents can spend.

The child sometimes becomes resentful at being awakened.

Because of the inconveniences and annoyances involved in the pad-and-buzzer method, many parents stop using it before success has been achieved. In some studies, as many as 40 percent of the parents discontinued the procedure. Had they continued, they might well have been successful, but they apparently became discouraged by the time, effort, and annoyance in this otherwise very effective method.

3 How the New Method Was Developed

Daytime Toilet Training

The origin of the new method of bedwetting treatment is similar to the origin of the new method of daytime toilet training which the senior author had designed earlier. Many readers may be familiar with the training manual entitled *Toilet Training in Less Than a Day* by N. H. Azrin and R. M. Foxx, which describes a rapid method of teaching young children how to toilet themselves. That book describes how toilet training was studied as part of a research effort to teach very severely retarded persons how to stop pants-wetting. When a method was discovered which was successful in one week, on average, with the severely retarded persons, the possibility seemed open that a modified version might be even more successful in teaching normal, nonretarded children to stop pants-wetting in even less time. The resulting research led to a method that was effective in one day for the average

31

child. The results were published in a psychological journal, have since been repeated by other investigators, and were described in the book mentioned above so that parents could learn about the procedure.

Treating Bedwetting of Retarded Persons

Profoundly retarded persons usually continue to wet their bed during their entire lives. Only a small number, perhaps 30 percent, ever learn how to control their wetting at night. The pad-and-buzzer procedure, which is so effective with nonretarded persons, was almost totally ineffective for profoundly retarded persons. Under the direction of the senior author, N. H. Azrin, a new method was developed, therefore, based on learning principles which used the pad-and-buzzer method but also taught the persons to awaken at night when necessary, to be very aware of the wet or dry state of their bed, to take personal responsibility for bedwetting, to become well-practiced in toileting at night, and to be strongly motivated to remain dry at night. The results were very favorable in that all of the retarded persons stopped bedwetting. The bedwetting accidents were decreased by 91 percent during the very first week, and by 95 percent after one month. The speed of the training was especially impressive when one considers the degree of impairment of the trainees. They were unable to speak, or to dress themselves, or to eat normally, or to understand normal speech. Most had serious physical disabilities as well, including partial deafness, or blindness, or paralysis of an arm or leg. All had reached adulthood, the youngest being twenty-five and the oldest, sixty-three. Yet all were still wetting their bed until they were trained by the new method.

Extending the New Method to Normal Children

If the new training method was successful in teaching the profoundly retarded adults, might it not be at least as effective for normal, nonretarded children? The method was modified so that it would take advantage of the language, understanding, and motivation of normal children, and then a clinical test was conducted. The procedure still included the pad-and-buzzer apparatus, but now stressed having the child understand and rehearse the actions he should take when he had the urge to urinate while in bed. The instructor stayed up with the child all night, awakening the child each hour to focus his attention on his bladder sensations. After the one night of intensive training, the parents maintained a schedule of praise, practice, and teaching of personal responsibility by the child. Twenty-six children were in the study, their ages ranging from three years old to fourteen years old. The new method produced a rapid interruption of the bedwetting. The average child had only two bedwetting accidents before achieving two weeks of uninterrupted dryness. All twenty-six children stopped bedwetting; there were no failures. In contrast, those children in the experiment who received normal pad-and-buzzer training had a much higher frequency of accidents during the first weeks. The new method was faster than the pad-and-buzzer apparatus.

We attempted to improve the new method still further. Not much room was left for improvement in terms of speed since the average child who had been wetting almost every night had only two accidents after the intensive training and then enjoyed two consecutive weeks of dryness. But, we could try to improve the convenience of the method since it required the child to be awakened every hour during the one night of intensive training. Also, the new method used the pad-and-buzzer apparatus which, as we discussed earlier, caused reluctance and annoyance in many parents. To eliminate these inconveniences, we devised an improved method which did not include the pad-and-buzzer apparatus and did not require the parents to stay up throughout the intensive training night, but only up to their normal bedtime—about midnight. To compensate for the loss of effectiveness that would result from these omissions, we added several procedures. First, we had the child rehearse during the day, when it was convenient for the parent. Second, we had the child practice each day, increasing the capacity of the bladder. Third, we added one nightly awakening at a time convenient for the parent so the child would experience success at the start of the training.

The results of the field test with fifty-four children showed that the parents strongly preferred the new method to the pad-and-buzzer treatment, all parents having been given the choice of or experience with both methods. Specifically, 85 percent of the parents who had first tried the pad and buzzer chose to change to the improved method after two weeks. Conversely, none of the parents who tried the improved method initially changed to the pad and buzzer when given the choice at the same time. The improved method was much preferred and still very effective. The results showed that the average child had only four accidents before achieving the standard of two consecutive weeks of dryness. On the very first day after the one day of intensive training, bedwetting was reduced by 70 percent. After one week, accidents were reduced by 80 percent and by 90 percent after four weeks. Follow-up after one year showed that bedwetting was reduced by 98 percent. The improved method without the pad-and-buzzer apparatus was slightly less effective than when the apparatus was included, but was still effective for all of the children, and within a few days and more rapid than alternative treatments. The slight loss of effectiveness of the improvements was balanced by a considerable gain in convenience.

Teaching Parents to Use the New Method

In the controlled experiments that tested the new method, a counselor had gone to the child's home to conduct the intensive training on the first day. Would the new method still be effective if the parents did the training alone? To answer this question, parents and their bedwetting children were given instruction in the office for one session lasting about one and a half hours, after which they went home to try the new method. The results showed that parents could use the new method successfully and achieve their objective quickly. Of the forty-four bedwetting children, all of them stopped wetting. The average reduction after one day was 80 percent, after one week, 84 percent, and 96 percent after four months. The average child had only four accidents before reaching the standard of two weeks of uninterrupted dryness. These results are almost the same as were obtained when the counselor conducted the training. This clinical trial assured us that parents could use the procedure after they and their child received a description and written instructions.

Why Was This Book Written?

This book represents the latest phase in the attempt to provide help to bedwetting children and their parents. The results of the experiments with this new method have been published in psychological journals where they will be read and eventually used by psychologists and medical doctors. But, not all parents of bedwetting children seek out professional help since such assistance is costly and not always easily available. Also, we have described how embarrassed many parents and children are about the failure of the child to stop bedwetting, and their resulting reluctance to seek professional help. By describing the new procedure in detail in an easily available book, we hope that many more parents will learn how to solve the bedwetting problem. For those who do seek out professional help, this book can still be of assistance to parents and children in achieving a greater understanding of the bedwetting problem and the details of the treatment. We hope that this book will bring us closer to the ideal of eliminating bedwetting for all children.

The final step was to determine whether parents could train their children successfully with the new method if no professional counseling were available, using only an instructional manual. We, therefore, wrote the present book to describe the details of the new method as well as its general rationale. When parents requested treatment for their child's bedwetting, they were given the training manual and asked to read it and to try the new method on their own without the detailed description and practice which had been provided by the counselor in the previous studies. A brief test was given to the parents to assure that they understood the procedure before attempting training. The results of this effort have not yet been written up and published in a psychological research journal, as the other studies have been, but the general outcome was fairly favorable. About 80 percent of the parents were successful in training their child after having read the training manual and without professional assistance. The remaining parents requested, or required, assistance in order to be successful. These results, taken together with the results of the previous studies, indicate that the new method is effective in reducing bedwetting quickly and substantially and that most parents can be successful after having read about, and carried out, the procedures described in this book.

How Many Children Were Used in Testing the Method?

Twenty-six children were treated in the first published study which used the buzzer apparatus. Fifty-four were used in the second study which omitted the apparatus. An additional forty-four children and their parents were taught in the third study in the office setting. About fifty other children were treated in developing procedural improvements and who were not included in the published studies. The total is about 175 children who have been treated by this general method.

Here we have described only briefly the general rationale of the method. In the next chapter we now examine this rationale and general plan in more detail.

4 General Plan and Rationale of Treatment

The various procedures in the new treatment method are based on an analysis of the bedwetting problem in terms of learning principles. We assume that the child has learned to toilet properly during the day and no longer wets his pants, but still wets the bed.

Awareness During Sleep

The principal reason for bedwetting seems to be simply that when the child is sound asleep he is naturally not as aware of his bladder sensations as he is when awake. The problem is not that the child sleeps too soundly, but rather that he lacks sufficient awareness such as mothers have who will easily awaken from a very sound sleep as soon as their baby cries because of the unconscious concentration on the sounds the baby is making. To increase this awareness of his bladder sensations, several procedures are used. The child is awakened several times on the first night and asked to describe his need to urinate. During the day, he lies down on his bed, imagines he is sleeping, describes whether he has the need to urinate, and states what he should do about it. The pad-and-buzzer apparatus, if used, will also alert him immediately to his urinary urges during sleep.

Increasing Bladder Control

A second reason for bedwetting is that bladder control is insufficiently developed. During the day when the child is awake, the bladder control may be sufficient, but at night, the lack of attention during sleep means that this borderline degree of bladder control will not be sufficient. To increase voluntary bladder control, the child practices during the day how to start urination and how to hold it back. He also practices holding urination back as long as possible so that the bladder capacity will be increased. The child keeps a record of his bladder capacity, and the parent encourages his progress in increasing it.

Practice in Nighttime Toileting

Assuming that a child has become aware of the need to urinate at night but as yet has insufficient bladder control to hold it back, he should, of course, arise from his bed and go to the family toilet. Yet, he may well be reluctant to do so either because he does not wish to disturb his sleep, the effort seems too great, or he is somewhat uncertain as to how to reach the toilet in the darkened house. The solution is to give the child extensive practice in arising from the bed to go to the toilet until the action becomes a strong habit which will occur even in a state of extreme drowsiness.

Immediate Success

Learning is more pleasant and more assured when some success occurs from the very beginning. Several procedures are included to create this immediate success. The first day of training is made very intensive so that all of the skills are learned at the beginning. Also, the child drinks large amounts of fluids on this first day so that he can have many practice trials on the correct way to react to the nighttime urge to urinate. To help the child go through the entire night without wetting even though his bladder control is still borderline, he is awakened to toilet during the first few nights so that he need only hold back the urine for part of the night. These awakenings are gradually omitted as the child demonstrates bladder control.

Accepting Personal Responsibility for Correcting Bedwetting

Bedwetting is similar to any other undesired behavior in that it often persists because we have resigned ourselves to the inconvenience, or have forgotten about the benefits of changing it. This situation is especially true when some other person, such as the mother, takes on the responsibility of correcting the inconveniences. The result then is that the mother becomes very annoyed. The solution in the new method is to have the child take responsibility himself for the inconveniences of bedwetting, and for practicing the skills necessary to prevent future accidents. The child, not the parent, changes the bed sheets and makes up the bed. Also, before training, the child reviews the inconveniences bedwetting has caused him. To emphasize the benefits of staying dry, the parent and child decide on exactly what benefits he will obtain when dryness has occurred. When accidents do occur, the child practices as soon as possible the skills that will prevent future accidents. The child and not the parent has the primary responsibility for keeping the progress charts. By giving the child the responsibility for correcting and practicing, the parent no longer suffers the many inconveniences and has less reason to be angry with the child. Conversely, the child realizes how important it is for him and will try harder to practice the preventive procedures on his own with minimal reminders. The parent can now concentrate on encouraging the child in his efforts. This viewpoint was illustrated during the counseling sessions in which the counselor first taught the child what to do. The parents were then called in and the child explained to the parents what was to be done and asked the parents to assist and remind him.

5 | Preparation for Training

How Old Should the Child Be?

Your child should be at least three years old. Children vary in their physical and mental development, but even if your two-year-old child seems advanced for his age, you should wait until the third birthday to give him an extra advantage.

Daytime Pants-wetting

If your child is still wetting his pants during the day, do not start bedwetting training. Wait until he has demonstrated perfect control during the day. Your child is definitely not ready if diapers are still being worn—in which case you should first toilet-train your child. A rapid

Before training for bedwetting, a child should be three years old and be able to stay dry during the day.

method for daytime toilet training is described in *Toilet Training in Less Than a Day*. If your child still has an occasional daytime pants-wetting, even once a month, delay starting the bedwetting training until at least a month has passed, and concentrate on teaching daytime control. Observe whether your child urinates very frequently during the day even if no pants-wettings occur, since a high frequency often indicates that the bladder capacity is not fully developed. If he must urinate every hour or two, start encouraging him to wait for longer

44

periods, until he is able to wait easily for three hours or more. In summary, your child is probably ready if he is three years old, has not had a pants-wetting accident during the past month, and can easily wait about three hours between toiletings.

Medical Problems

If your child is ill, he should be treated for the illness before considering bedwetting training. Even if he has only a cold, wait until he has recovered, and do the same if he seems especially tired or listless or has any unusual physical complaints such as a headache or stomachache. Only a very small percentage—about 2 percent—of bedwetting cases are caused by a medical problem, but if you suspect a medical cause, secure medical treatment, especially if urination is painful. If your child has epilepsy, you should not give excessive fluids, so omit that aspect of the procedure. Also, do not use drinks or snacks containing sugar if your child is diabetic. In general, exercise the same precautions you normally do regarding your child's medical needs and consult your physician if there is any doubt.

Drink and Snack Treats

If your child is young, three to eight years, you will be using snacks as part of your demonstration of approval. For children of all ages, you will be giving many drinks on the first day to create a strong desire to urinate so that your child will have more practice trials on the correct way to deal with these urges. For the younger children,

The child drinks lots of liquids so he will have a strong urge to urinate during training and be able to practice controlling that urge.

the drinks are also used as a reward. At the start of training, have several types of drinks available, selecting those that you know are his favorites, such as milk, soda, punch, cocoa, and juices—but not juice and milk too close together, since this combination upsets the digestion of some children. Similarly, have favorite snack treats such as potato chips, pretzels, raisins, pieces of fruit, dry cereal on hand for the younger child. Of course, include only those items that you feel that your child should have.

Have these snack items conveniently available, preferably in a large pocket, or if that is not feasible, on a high counter top near you.

Where to Train

Training will occur in the child's bedroom and in the toilet. Since your child will be traveling frequently between these two rooms, a special problem may occur for very young children when the bathroom is on a different level of the house and they cannot climb the stairs easily. One solution is to leave the child's potty-chair in his bedroom at night if he is still young enough to use one. A second solution is to give your child guided practice in using the stairs until you feel comfortable that he can do so safely by himself at night. If so, you will want to leave a light on at night to illuminate the stairs. For children of all ages, provide a dim night-light in the bedroom and in the hall leading to the bathroom so that your child can see well enough to find his way there. These lights should be very dim since the eye becomes sensitive during sleep and bright lights will be annoyingly intense upon awakening and will interfere with sleep.

Bed Arrangements

Your child should have his own bed and the bed should be arranged and located so that he can easily climb out of it and he can replace the sheets comfortably. If he is still in a crib type of bed, with a sliding side rail, lower the rail as far as possible so that it will not prevent him from climbing out. If your child is very young and you are concerned about him falling out, leave the rail just high enough to prevent this, but still low enough for him to climb over easily. Also, the mattress level must be low enough so that your child can step down easily to the floor. If you have an adjustable level for the spring and mattress, as is common on most cribs, lower the spring to the lowest level provided. If the mattress level is uncomfortably high and cannot be lowered, as in a regular bed, place a wide, stable stool, bench, box, or other object on the floor next to the bed so he can step down on it. Another consideration is that the bed should be at least a foot away from the walls on all sides to allow the sheets to be changed easily by your child when an accident has occurred. Some dry sheets should be in a location that your child can reach easily so he can obtain them without your assistance.

Ideally, your child should have his own bedroom so that his brothers and sisters will not be disturbed by his practicing. If he shares his bedroom with others, the disturbance will be reduced if his bed is the nearest to the door leading to the toilet.

More Than One Bedwetter in the Family

If two or more of your children are wetting their beds, start training with your oldest bedwetter. After your oldest child has stopped wetting for at least three weeks, you can start with your younger child. Your older child should then assist the younger one and will probably be eager to do so. Allow the younger bedwetting child to observe the older child's training since this promotes learning by imitation and he may become dry as a result of this observation.

One Child Is Wetting, but the Others Are Not

Children can be cruel to a brother or sister who is bed-wetting when the other children do not have the problem. Accordingly, the brothers and sisters should be told about the training effort and their support should be encouraged. Otherwise, they may well interfere with your efforts. Tell them what you and their sibling will be doing beforehand, and have them tell you how they will react so you are sure that they understand.

Let Your Child Read About the Program

If your child is old enough to do so, have him read this book beforehand so that he also will be familiar with the details before you start the training. Ask him to put a written mark at any page or section he does not understand so that you can explain it to him later and discuss any other questions as well. Even if your child is fairly young and does not read too well, you can still use this book. Chapter 10 is a story about a boy who was taught to stop bedwetting. For a younger child, you should read this to him as a bedtime story.

Pad-and-Buzzer Apparatus

The pad-and-buzzer apparatus is included in the present procedure as an optional one. As was discussed in Chapter 2, this apparatus will make learning more rapid, but

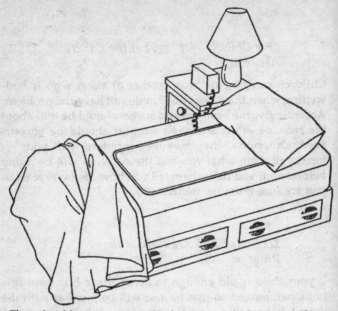

The pad-and-buzzer apparatus signals as soon as the bed is wet. This apparatus is slightly inconvenient but helps in learning to stay dry.

some parents say that they would rather not use it. The present method will take slightly longer if the pad and buzzer are not used, and consequently that is why the apparatus is recommended. Remember that the test results showed that the average bedwetter had only two instances of bedwetting, and accordingly there would be only two nights when the buzzer sounded, before two consecutive weeks of dryness occurred during which, of course, the buzzer never sounded. Because this method is so rapid, very few bedwettings will occur, and very few buzzer soundings, and very infrequent interruptions of the parents' sleep. On the other hand, you personally may still not desire to use the apparatus either because of this annoyance, or cost, or unavailability, or for any other reason.

If your decision is to omit the apparatus, skip all of the descriptions of its use in the remainder of this book.

If you have decided to use the apparatus, obtain one before starting this program. At the time of writing this book, the apparatus was advertised as available from the companies that are listed in Appendix 5. No endorsement is intended of either of these companies, the list being included to provide you with a choice and since the suppliers of this type of apparatus might be difficult for you to locate. No description will be given here as to how to operate the apparatus, since the operating procedure differs from one type to another and since each type of apparatus usually is accompanied by clear instructions specific to that model. The apparatuses have usually been certified as to safety and are probably no less safe than the electric blankets widely used for warmth.

There are some general rules for proper use of the pad-and-buzzer apparatus whatever model is obtained. You and your child should both examine the apparatus at each bedtime to be certain that it is connected properly. If the apparatus requires replacement pads, obtain an adequate supply beforehand. At each bedtime, locate the pad in the central area of the bed where your child's hips are most likely to be located. Locate the buzzer-off switch far enough from the bed so that your child will not simply reach out and shut off the buzzer while still half asleep. In hot weather, avoid excessive night clothing or blankets which will cause the buzzer to sound because of perspiration. If another child is in the same room, avoid use of a model that illuminates a lamp light in addition to sounding a buzzer. When the buzzer sounds, try to go to your child as soon as possible to help him awaken; otherwise he will become accustomed to sleeping through the buzzer.

Measuring Cup

Your child will be using a measuring cup in which to urinate as part of the program to increase the capacity of the bladder. Before training, obtain a widemouthed and transparent cup which is graduated in units of ½ ounces and has a total capacity of 16 ounces. The gradations should be clearly marked so that your child can read them easily, and the cup should be transparent so that small units of progress can be readily seen. The cup should be kept in the bathroom where your child can reach it easily.

Calendar Progress Chart

Post a chart of your child's progress in his room so that he can see at a glance how many dry nights he has had. Obtain beforehand a calendar which is large enough to be seen easily from a distance and post it on the wall at a height at which it is convenient for him to write—about shoulder-high for him. Instead of a calendar, you may use the calendar-type charts included in Appendix 7, which you can tear out. Alternatively, you may prefer to make up your own calendar form on a larger sheet of paper. Leave a pencil or pen near the chart, or preferably tied to a string and fastened nearby so that it will always be at hand.

What Day Should You Choose for Training?

If your child is attending school, it is possible to start the training when he returns from school if he comes home in the early afternoon. If you are a working parent and are not home during the day, training is best done on a week-end or a nonworking day. Most nonworking parents have preferred Friday afternoon and evening, whereas working parents have preferred Saturday or Sunday. The general guideline is to select a day when you can start training about 4:00 P.M. and have the entire evening free from visitors or competing activities. To avoid interruption of the new program, a date should be selected when the parents and child do not expect to take a vacation for at least a month. A vacation away from home during the first month would mean a change of bedtime and toileting schedules which could interrupt progress.

Both Parents

Both parents should be familiar with the training program and, if agreeable, both parents can participate in training although that is not necessary. If either parent does not desire to use the pad-and-buzzer apparatus, do not use it. If one parent is away from home for a few days, wait until both are present. If one parent is reluctant to use this training program, these doubts will probably be conveyed to the child, so such doubts should be resolved first so that each parent will be supportive of the efforts of the child and other parent.

Nightclothes

If your child is very young, he should wear loosely fitting training pants or pajamas which can be lowered easily for toileting. If your child is so young that he wears diapers in bed, discontinue the diapers since they are too difficult for him to remove himself.

Benefits of Being Dry at Night

About one day before training, review with your child the various benefits which will result from staying dry at night. Start by asking him what he doesn't like about wetting the bed and "What nice things could you do?" when he no longer wets at night.

As a reminder to your child, you may use the following list of reasons offered by many children of what they don't like about bedwetting. Review each item and check it off if it applies to your child.

_____ *Teasing* by brothers or sisters or friends.

_____ *Camp.* Can't go to summer camp.

_____ *Overnight at friend's house.* Afraid to wet their bed.

_____ *Friends overnight at my house.* Afraid they'll find out I wet.

_____ *Self-respect.* I feel ashamed of myself.

_____ *Parents annoyed.* Parents are disappointed and wetting causes work.

_____ *Camping overnight.* Can't have a sleeping bag for overnight camping.

_____ *Skin rash* from sleeping in wet pajamas and pants.

_____ *Visiting relatives overnight.* My parents are ashamed to let their relatives know.

_____ *Other.*

FOR VERY YOUNG CHILDREN

_____ *Bed instead of a crib.* Regular bed to replace the crib.

_____ *No diapers at night.* Training pants instead of diapers.

_____ *Grown-up.* Not be a baby anymore.

_____ *Other.*

Agreement for Benefits for Staying Dry

We want your child to enjoy immediately the natural benefits of staying dry at night. After you have reviewed the benefits in the previous list that your child desires, make a firm agreement the day before starting training about what specific benefits you will provide and when you will provide them. Use the benefits checked in the previous list as a guide. For example, if your child indicated he would like to have a friend overnight, make an agreement that you will allow him to have a friend overnight (specify whom), and on what day, and after how many consecutive days of dryness. The statement should be written out so that it will remind you and your child at the later date of the benefits to be received, since the details can easily be forgotten. A sample statement might be: Billy can call a friend up (Mike, Frank, or Charlie) to stay overnight on a Friday or Saturday night when five straight nights have passed without wetting. If too many straight dry nights are required, then the benefits will be too far away in time to seem possible, so you should choose a number of straight dry nights that is as small as possible, yet is reasonable. As to the selection of benefits, do not use only artificial rewards such as an increased allowance or movies which are not natural benefits for dryness. Only for young children, perhaps three to eight years of age, should many artificial benefits be used, since the natural benefits are not as real for them at that age.

To assist you in making these agreements, two sample agreement forms are presented, one for a four-year-old child and one for a thirteen-year-old child.

As noted in the agreement forms, artificial rewards such as the snacks and toys are used more for the younger child than for the older one, especially for the first few nights of dryness. Several other features of both contracts are important. Some benefits are scheduled for even one, two, or three nights of dryness so that the satisfactions will occur quickly. The exact number of nights of dryness is always specified to eliminate vagueness as to what is desired. The description of the benefit is always very specific so the child knows exactly what to look forward to. The agreements always specify an immediate action that the parent will take to schedule the benefit when the specified number of dry nights is achieved even if the benefit will occur later. Your child will be more successful and more motivated if the agreements you make with him contain these features.

SAMPLE AGREEMENT FORM
FOR A FOUR-YEAR-OLD GIRL—SANDRA

Special Treat No. 1: When Sandra has her first dry night, we will buy her a banana split the next day.

Special Treat No. 2: When Sandra has two dry nights, we will buy her the robot set she wants.

Special Treat No. 3: When Sandra has three dry nights, we will bake her a cake the next day.

Diapers: When Sandra has had five days without wetting a single night, we will throw all her diapers away and use them as rags.

Bed: When Sandra has had two weeks without a single wetting, we will go to the furniture store and buy her a grown-up bed like Mary's (her neighbor) and put the crib away in the basement.

Visit Grandma: When Sandra has had three weeks without wetting, we will call Grandma and ask her to have Sandra visit overnight.

SAMPLE AGREEMENT FORM
FOR A FOURTEEN-YEAR-OLD BOY (BOBBY)

Special Treat No. 1: When Bobby has his first dry night, we will treat him to any item of his choice at the ice cream stand on the next day.

Special Treat No. 2: When Bobby has three straight dry nights, we will get him the football he wants at the sports store the next day.

Sleeping Bag: After one week of dry nights, we will buy Bobby a sleeping bag like the one on p. 300 of the camping catalog.

Friends Overnight: After ten days of dry nights, Bobby can call his friends over for a pajama party the next weekend we are home.

Visiting Friends: After two weeks of dry nights, Bobby can call a friend (Mickey, Doug, Ray, Tom) to stay at his house the next weekend.

Camping: After three weeks of dry nights, we will arrange a family camping trip for our next holiday.

Summer Camp: After four weeks of dry nights, we will enroll Bobby in Boy Scout Camp for three weeks.

The various decisions and preparations for training should be made together with the child and in the spirit of a game. Do not decide by yourself or prepare by yourself. Instead, shop with your child for the measuring cup, snacks, etc., and have him assist with the Calendar Progress Chart, bed arrangement, and, of course the agreements. In this way, we are making him an active participant rather than a spectator.

6 | The Intensive Training Day

This first day of training should start in the early afternoon, about 3:00 to 4:00 P.M. for school-age children, and will end at about midnight or 1:00 A.M. The later you stay up, the more likely your child will be off to a good start. If your child is a preschooler, start the training shortly after lunch. Once training starts, your child should remain in the house and not go outdoors, since he will be practicing toileting at frequent intervals. He may, however, engage in some of his usual indoor activities so long as he understands and agrees that these activities will be regularly interrupted. Similarly, you can usually engage in some of your normal indoor activities, such as reading, meal preparation, household tasks, talking to family members, so long as you give priority to the practice trials and interrupt these activities at the scheduled times. Do not schedule any outside activities, visits by others, long telephone calls, shopping trips, or any other events that will occupy your attention for more than a few minutes. The reason is that on the first training day you should spend as much time as possible with your child between practice trials discussing with him what he will be doing in each of the steps in training.

Drinking to Create Frequent Desire to Urinate

Have your child drink as much as he comfortably can so that he will have a strong desire to urinate and will be able to have intensive practice in how to control this urge. Start giving extra drinks at the very start of training and continue until two hours before the end of training, which should be about 10:00 or 11:00 P.M. if training ends at midnight or 1:00 A.M. Use a graduated measuring glass to serve the drinks so that you can keep track of the amount. If your child is very young, try to have him drink about one glass (eight ounces) every hour for the first few hours. But, the older child should drink about two glasses (sixteen ounces) every hour for the first few hours. If he can comfortably drink more, have him do so and actively encourage him to drink by offering the drinks to him every fifteen minutes. Salty snacks (potato chips, popcorn, pretzels, peanuts, corn chips) should be freely available to him all the time, and you should remind him to eat some about every fifteen minutes.

For very young children, encourage them in addition by slightly sipping some of the drink yourself and by holding it up to touch their lips and by presenting it as a game or contest to see how much they can drink. After the first few hours, your child will probably be able to drink less than before. By getting only favorite drinks and snacks, and being encouraged to consider this drinking a humorous game, your child will view it as pleasant and fun. Older children and young adults who normally drink coffee or tea are especially advised to do so here since these drinks have the special characteristic of promoting the urge to urinate.

These extra drinks are given only during the first day and night of training.

Training in "Holding Back"

Children who wet their bed have been found to have a smaller bladder capacity and to urinate more frequently during the day than nonbedwetters. The holding-back procedure helps to increase the ability of the bladder to hold more urine and for a longer time. The procedure also teaches your child to be very sensitive to his bladder feelings, especially while in bed. The child is taught to strain until he has the urge to urinate, then to lie down on his bed where he practices holding back as long as he can.

The holding-back training starts about half an hour after the first large amount of drink has been taken, since that is about when the bladder should be somewhat filled. At this time, have your child go to the bathroom to strain and try to urinate. Use whatever terms are common for you and appropriate to the child's age. "Betty, try to go to the toilet," or "Billy, try to pee-pee." Have them try until they have a "full feeling." When he does "feel like I have to go," or, "I feel full now," or, "I feel like pee-pee," tell him to "hold it back," to try *not* to urinate and have him go quickly to lie down on his bed. There he is to lie quietly and pretend he is asleep by closing his eyes and breathing slowly and deeply. Have him lie down for two minutes while you encourage him to hold back his urine.

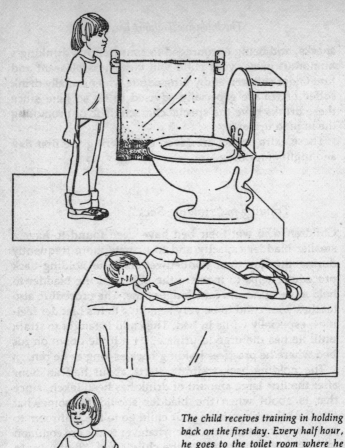

The child receives training in holding back on the first day. Every half hour, he goes to the toilet room where he strains until he feels an urge to urinate (top frame). When he feels this urge, he goes to his bed where he lies down, pretending sleep, and consciously holds back this urge (middle frame). After holding back for two minutes in bed, if he can, or rushing to the toilet if he can't hold back, he returns to playing (bottom frame) until the next practice.

If he is able to hold back for the two minutes and the urge is gone, he can return to his previous play activities. But if he says he cannot wait any longer, have him get up and rush to the toilet to urinate. If he is able to wait the two minutes but still has the urge at the end of that time, also have him get up then to go to the toilet. The sequence, in summary, is for the child to strain on the toilet every half hour until he has to urinate, at which time he goes to his bed and lies down and tries to hold back for two minutes. If the urge disappears, he returns to play. If the urge gets too strong, he rushes to the toilet. If the urge is still present after two minutes, he rushes to the toilet.

When the child is to arise from bed to go to the toilet, it is useful to prompt him with a phrase that emphasizes his active role, such as "Jump up and go."

Practice Every Half Hour

Repeat this holding-back practice every half hour from the start of training until bedtime. To help remind you and your child, it is more convenient to schedule it at the half hour and at the hour such as at 1:30, 2:00, 2:30, 3:00 . . . Another helpful reminder is to use a kitchen timer as a signal in which case your child will feel more personally responsible if you have him rather than you set it each time.

Unscheduled Toileting

Tell your child that if he has to go to the toilet before the next scheduled practice, he is to call you, at which time you will conduct the hold-back procedure in the same way as if it were scheduled. Then, consider that practice as a substitute for the next practice period.

Younger Children

Younger children usually require assistance in timing how long they are to hold back. While they are holding back in bed (eyes closed) have them count slowly to fifty, or to say the alphabet slowly, whichever is within their capability. Have them say it softly aloud at first so that you can provide help if necessary.

Discussing Procedure

While your young child is holding back in bed, have the child describe what should be done at the various stages of urgency, prompting when necessary. For example, you might say, "Marilyn, hold it back as long as you can. Now, think about how your tummy feels. When you are in bed and asleep and you have that full feeling, what will you do?"

"I'll hold it back for as long as I can. Until it goes away."

"Good! If it doesn't go away, what will you do then, Marilyn?"

"I'll get up out of bed, and I'll go fast to the bathroom so I won't wet the bed."

"That's good; you know exactly what to do. Now pretend you are sound asleep, but think hard about how your tummy feels. You have done beautifully! Only one minute longer now."

When the child is holding back for two minutes in bed, continually remind the child to think of his full feeling, praise his success, and encourage him to continue. But do not request any lengthy replies, since he is to be in a very relaxed state.

As another example, the parent might say:

"Jimmy, think of your stomach. Think of how full it feels. Are you thinking of how your stomach feels?"

"Mhmm."

"Good, keep thinking of it. You have just a little longer to wait. I'm so happy you can wait so long. You can do it at night, too, I'm sure of that."

"I finished counting."

"Do you still have to go?"

"Yes."

"OK, do what you will do at night when you still have to go."

"I jump up out of bed and go to the bathroom so I won't wet the bed."

"You know just what to do. Hurry. I've got the candy and drinks waiting as soon as you finish. Jump up and go."

By engaging in these descriptions, you are assuring that your child is developing a heightened sensitivity to the state of the bladder. These descriptions should continue during each of the practice periods every half hour.

Increasing the Duration of Holding Back

The duration of holding back should be lengthened gradually from one practice period to the next. Start with the two-minute goal on the first trial and increase it by one minute each time as the child succeeds. If the time goal proves to be too long on a trial, keep it at the same duration, or even decrease it slightly, on the next trial until your child has been successful, treating the experience as a game in which you are trying to set a record. To keep track of the times, it is convenient to keep a paper and pen or pencil in the bathroom and write down the durations achieved on each effort so that you can know what goal to set next time as well as to be able to review the progress with your child at each practice period.

Early Bedtime

The holding-back practice will have been conducted several times, once every half hour. Bedtime on this training day should be set slightly earlier than usual, preferably no later than 7:00 P.M. for younger children and 8:00 P.M. for older children and young adults so that more time will be spent on actual sleep-time practice.

Changing Bed Sheets

Explain to your child that he will be taking personal responsibility for changing the bed sheets from now on and cleaning up when an accident occurs. One hour before bedtime, teach him how to change the bed sheets. First, demonstrate by doing it yourself while he observes, then have him do it while you watch him, being careful that he does all of it himself, including obtaining the fresh sheets and putting the old ones in the laundry hamper. For very young children, many parents have had doubts that their three- or four-year-old could change the sheets alone, but our experience has been that they can do so under patient, guided instructions. The general rule is to

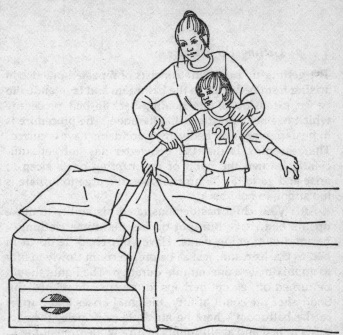

The child is taught to make his bed so he can take responsibility for correcting any future bedwettings.

describe each move in detail when you demonstrate and to guide the child's hands manually as soon as he has difficulty in doing it himself, praising him continuously for his efforts. The younger children should be asked to make up the bed two or three times if great difficulty was experienced on the first attempt. Generally, even the youngest child has been delighted with this adult responsibility and pleased to be able to remove this source of annoyance for the parents.

Getting-Up Practice

The getting-up procedure consists of repeated practice in arising from bed to go to the bathroom and is intended to be an extension of the holding-back-in-bed procedure which has been practiced all afternoon. The procedure is to be used whenever bedwetting accidents have occurred. The reasoning is that the bedwetter has not yet sufficiently learned the habit of interrupting one's sleep to arise and go to the bathroom when the urge to urinate is too strong to hold back.

After your child has demonstrated his ability to make up the bed, have him put on his nighttime clothing—pajamas or training pants. Have your child lie down in bed as if asleep and, just as before, to count slowly to fifty to approximate a one-minute duration. The lights should be turned off, except perhaps for a very dim night-light. Soon after the count of fifty, the child arises and hurries to the bathroom where he attempts to urinate, then returns to bed and again counts to fifty while pretending to be asleep. This sequence is repeated twenty times; that is, he has lain in bed for twenty one-minute periods and practiced getting up from this imagined sleep to go to the bathroom. The total duration will be about one half hour.

Explain to your child the reasoning behind this getting-up practice beforehand, and explain that he will be doing this when an accident occurs so that more accidents will be prevented.

As your child does the getting-up practice, remain close by him, staying in the bedroom when he is in bed and walking directly behind him as he goes to the bathroom.

Bedtime Reminders

When your child goes to bed at the early bedtime, review the various features of the training program. Have your child describe to you what he is expected to do tonight if he feels the urge to urinate. "Hold it back. Or, jump up and go to the bathroom." Review what the agreed-upon benefits will be if he stays dry. Have him describe, say, who will change the bed if there is an accident and how he will do the getting-up practice. Explain to him that you will be waking him up a few times tonight to ask him about his need to toilet. Remind him to keep thinking about how his bladder feels. Have him touch and stroke the sheets and comment on their dryness. Strongly assure him of your confidence in his ability to stay dry on the basis of how well he has been able to hold back urination for long periods in his practice trials that day.

Hourly Awakenings During Sleep

After your child has gone to bed about 7:00 to 8:00 P.M. on this first training day, you will awaken him every hour until about midnight or 1:00 A.M. The purpose of these awakenings is similar to the holding-back practice trials he has been receiving that day prior to bedtime. Namely, he is learning to become very sensitive and alert to the full bladder feelings, to practice holding back, to practice getting up to go to the toilet but now doing so while actually in bed.

At each hourly awakening time, first feel the sheets to determine if they are dry. If they are dry, awaken him as gently as possible since we wish him to learn to awaken

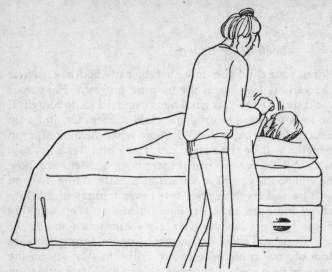

On the first training night, the child is awakened every hour until 1:00 A.M. to teach him to wake up easily.

with minimal prompting. First, call his name, then touch his shoulder while talking to him, then help him raise himself to a seated position until he is sitting without assistance. Ask him whether he has the full feeling in his stomach, and whether he must go to the toilet or whether he can wait until the next hour. If he says he can wait, praise him for his control, have him feel the sheets for their dryness, remind him to keep thinking about the full feeling, give him some more drinks, and have him return to sleep. As stated previously, the drinks are not given during the last two awakening trials, but are given during all of the earlier awakening trials.

If, upon being awakened, your child says he cannot

wait another hour, have him quickly jump up and go to the bathroom to urinate while you follow behind. When he has finished and returned to his bed, praise him for getting up, have him feel the sheets for dryness, remind him to keep thinking about the full feeling, give him some more drinks, and have him return to sleep for another hour.

Bedwetting Accident During Training Night

If you find the sheets are wet when you feel them at the hourly inspection, awaken your child so that he can change the sheets and do the getting-up practice. First, tell him that you are disappointed that the sheets are wet and have him feel them for wetness himself. Then have him obtain fresh nightclothes, put the wet clothing in the hamper himself, and dress himself. Then have him change the sheets just as he had practiced doing before bedtime. He removes the wet sheets himself, puts them in the laundry hamper, obtains the dry sheets, and puts them on the bed himself.

After the bed is remade, have him do the getting-up practice for twenty trials, just as he had done before bedtime. He lies down in his bed for about one minute, counting slowly to fifty, arises quickly, and rushes to the bathroom to try to toilet, and then returns to bed, repeating this sequence for twenty trials. When he has finished, he returns to bed. No further drinks are given. Ask him to feel the sheets for their dryness, remind him to think harder about his full feeling, and praise him for cleaning up and for the getting-up practice. Also remind him that he will be doing the getting-up practice again before bedtime tomorrow to help him prevent further accidents. Reassure him of your confidence that he will be dry at the next inspection an hour later.

Keep conversation and praise to a minimum while your child is changing his clothes and the sheets and doing the getting-up practice. Otherwise, for the younger child especially, cleaning up and practicing after an accident can become so entertaining that he may be tempted to have accidents deliberately. Conversely, if there is continuing criticism and scolding, the child is likely to become very upset. The solution is to keep a middle ground and neutral attitude which is neither showing pleasure nor anger, but rather is an attitude that a problem has occurred about which you and your child have an understanding that he will correct. So, it is very important that you had discussed and he had agreed beforehand, prior to training, that he would take the responsibility willingly to change his clothing and sheets himself and practice the getting-up trials. So, when your child has an accident, you should first let him take the initiative. If he does not, give only a general reminder: "Timmy, the bed is wet. You know what to do now when it is wet." If he does not start or tell you what he is to do, make a simple informational statement, such as, "Put on dry clothes," or "Take off the wet sheets," or "When you wet, you change your clothes and sheets." Do not lecture or give long explanations.

Manual Guidance

For the younger child who is unsure of his skill in changing his clothes and sheets, gentle manual guidance is necessary. Within one or two seconds after giving your instruction, touch his hands and guide them through the correct actions. Release your touch after a second or two, and if he is making an effort, do not provide further manual guidance. If he stops, touch and, if necessary, guide briefly again. Stand next to, or right behind, your young child as he cleans up so that when you give an instruction you can touch and guide him immediately if he hesitates. Do not give an instruction if you are more than two feet away and certainly not from the other side of the room. For the older children, this manual guidance is usually not necessary or useful, but you should still stand close by the first time cleaning up is necessary so that you can give instructions if needed as to how you want the bed made. Also, during the getting-up practice, you may need to give instructions to him to count to the full count of fifty, to do so slowly, and to hurry to the bathroom rather than walking very slowly.

Bedwetting Signaled by Buzzer

If the pad-and-buzzer apparatus is properly functioning, a bedwetting accident would be signaled immediately by the buzzer. If the sheets were found to be wet at the hourly inspection, then the apparatus could not have been functioning properly and you should determine whether it has been hooked up correctly so that it will signal wetting next time. If a bedwetting is signaled by the buzzer, follow the same procedure described above for bedwettings discovered by inspection. That is, have your child change the bed, change his clothes, practice the getting-up actions for twenty trials, and give him all of the other reminders mentioned before.

Reset the apparatus following the instructions of the manufacturer.

The next awakening should be one hour after the bed-wetting accident signaled by the buzzer.

Ending the First Training Night

The extra drinks will have been given all afternoon as well as during the period before bedtime, and at the hourly awakenings. Two hours before the last awakening, discontinue the drinks. Otherwise your child will have so much fluid that he will not be able to keep from bedwetting. So, if the last awakening is at 1:00 A.M., give drinks at the eleven o'clock awakening but not at the awakenings at midnight or at 1:00 A.M. Also, most children are not able to drink as much at the early awakenings as they had during the afternoon, so do not force the child to drink more than he can even if it is only a few ounces.

Awakening your child should become easier after he becomes accustomed to it. On the first or second awakening, you may need to hold him up in the sitting position for a few minutes until he is fully alert, but on successive awakenings, he should be able to awaken with only slight guidance.

After the last awakening, check that the buzzer apparatus, if you are using one, is set properly before you go to bed yourself.

In practice, almost none of the children have had an accident during the first night even though they have had so much to drink. The reasons are that they are awakened every hour and toilet themselves if they have the need, and also have their attention focused so strongly on their bladder sensations, the dry state of their bed sheets, and on the advantages of staying dry at night. All of these factors have come about because of the effort you and your child have made during the first day of intensive training. Your child is off to a good start, having been successful on this very first night even after having had more to drink than he has ever had before bedtime.

7 | Procedure After the First Training Day

General Plan

On the first day of training, your child learned about all of the procedures that he will now use on a less concentrated basis. Some of the procedures used on the first day will not be used again. The extra drinks are given only on the first day and not thereafter. Also, the awakenings every hour at night happen only on the first night, but thereafter only one awakening occurs each night, and even that one is eliminated after a short while as will be described shortly. The strain-and-hold procedure used every half hour on the first day will no longer be used. Instead, a modified procedure will be used to increase your child's bladder capacity whereby your child will attempt on his own to urinate less frequently in that he urinates only when his bladder is very full. Your child will continue to assume responsibility for his bedwettings by changing himself and the bed when an accident

75

occurs and also to practice the getting-up procedure. If it was used initially, the pad-and-buzzer apparatus will continue to be used to help him become aware of the moment when his bladder lets go. Having given this overview, we will now consider the specific procedures to be used after the first day of intensive training.

Increasing Bladder Capacity

The day after training starts, begin bladder training procedure. Leave the transparent graduated cup in the bathroom in a place convenient for your child and have him urinate only into that container and not into the toilet. He is to use the graduated container whenever he urinates when at home. After each urination, read the number of ounces from the gradations on the container and write it down on a piece of paper which should also be located in the bathroom with a pen or pencil. If your child is an older child, or is a young adult, he can record this information himself. If your child is young, he should call you or your spouse at the time he urinates, or shortly thereafter, so that you can read the amount and write it on the piece of paper.

Compare the amount that he just urinated with the amount urinated on previous attempts and on previous days. If the amount is greater than ever before, tell him so. "Jimmy, that's eight ounces! Wow, that's more than you ever did! Your bladder is getting very big." Even if the amount is not the largest, provide him with encouragement and favorable comparisons. Imagine your child on Monday had six ounces, four ounces, and seven ounces, and now on his next urination had five ounces, you could say "Five ounces, Jimmy, that's more than you did the second time this morning. That's getting better."

Every day, the child urinates into a measuring cup instead of in the toilet and tries to increase his bladder capacity.

Or "Five ounces this time. That's more than you did any-time on the first day you started. You're really trying. Let's see if you can set a record next time." Even if the amount is the lowest ever, a positive attitude can be ex-pressed. "Jimmy, it's only two ounces this time and that's not too high. But yesterday and this morning you had seven ounces, so I'd say you're doing great. Every day gets a little better. Let's try to make the next one extra big to make up for this one, OK?" Show this same positive attitude of encouragement for the older, as well as the younger child. Since the older child or young adult is recording himself, have him call you when he has finished urination to show you the container and to allow you to see the result compared with previous efforts.

The bladder control procedure is used until two weeks have passed without a single bedwetting accident. Then your child returns to urinating in the usual manner. As a way of reminding yourself and your child of this time requirement, you may add it to the list of agreements you had drawn up.

If your child is very young, be sure to give him a snack treat as well as praising him after any urination which is greater than the usual amount.

Allowance of Fluids

One of the most common methods of attempting to stop bedwetting is to prevent the child from drinking much fluid during the day and certainly none before bedtime. Yet, the evidence exists that this restriction of fluid is not helpful. When fluids have been restricted, the bladder capacity decreases and consequently the child is not able to retain as much fluid during the night. If the child is allowed, and encouraged, to drink freely during the day, the bladder capacity increases and the child is better able to sleep through the night without having to urinate. In the present method, large amounts of drinks were used during the first day only. After the first day, allow your child to drink fully and freely during the day, although do not encourage him to do so to the extent of the first day. Do not discourage him from drinking before bedtime either. Explain to your child that his bladder will get bigger and more used to holding liquids if he does drink freely during the day.

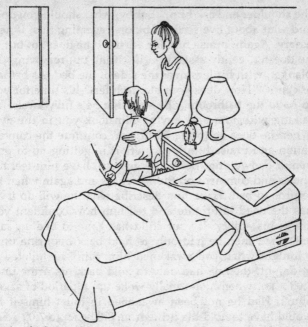

During the first week or two of training, the child gets up to toilet himself once during the early evening so he won't have to hold back the urine all night long. This is gradually phased out.

Nightly Awakening

On the second night of training, you will awaken your child once at your normal bedtime. So, if your normal bedtime is midnight, awaken your child then. Use the same gentle method of awakening you used for the hourly awakenings on the first training night. Tap your child on the shoulder and ask him, "Bobby, what should you do?" and wait about five seconds before repeating this, if necessary. Again, praise him for arising if he does so, but, if he doesn't, gently assist him in sitting up, removing the blanket, with his legs over the side of the bed. As before, ask him, "How does your stomach feel? It's time for you to go to the bathroom." Be sure that he's fully awake by talking with him and having him look you in the eye. When he does go to the bathroom, continue the conversation and praise him for his effort in getting up to prevent a bedwetting. Before he gets up, have him feel the sheets and comment on their dryness and again when he returns to bed. Have him describe what he will do if he has the need to urinate and tell him how confident you are in his ability. If your child has gone to bed at, say, 8:00 P.M., then he had only to hold back his urine until midnight when you awakened him. Since he toileted at midnight, then he had only to hold back his urine until 7:00 A.M., when he normally woke up, a period of seven hours. Had he not been awakened to toilet himself he would have to hold his urine from 8:00 P.M. to 7:00 A.M., a total of eleven hours.

Adjusting the Awakenings

The interval for which your child must hold back his urine is gradually increased each night that he is dry by awakening him a half hour earlier each night. So, in the above example, he is awakened at 11:30 the next night, then 11:00 the next, then 10:30, 10:00, 9:30, and so on. When the awakening time is only one hour after his bedtime, discontinue the nightly awakenings entirely. So, in the present example, when the awakening time reaches 9:00 P.M., omit the awakening since he had gone to bed only an hour previously and will not benefit appreciably by the awakening. Move the awakening time one half hour earlier as described each night for which your child was dry. But, if he was wet the previous night, keep the time of awakening the same until the next dry night occurs. So, if your child had been awakened at ten o'clock the night before and had a bedwetting that night, then tonight you will again awaken him at ten o'clock, not at nine thirty, and continue at ten o'clock until a dry night occurs. This adjusting schedule gradually increases the duration for which he must stay dry as long as he is successful. But when he has an accident, the duration does not increase. This schedule gradually moves the nightly awakening from the parents' normal bedtime closer to the child's normal bedtime.

Happy Clock

Use the "Happy Clock" as illustrated as a way of keeping track of the time that you should give the nightly awakening. A blank Happy Clock is included in Appendix 6, which you can tear out for use with your child, or draw your own on a larger sheet of paper which will be more clearly visible. Post the Happy Clock next to your child's bed so that both of you can look at it each bedtime to determine what time he should be awakened that night and to praise him for the progress toward eliminating the nightly awakening entirely.

The Happy Clock in the illustration has two hands penciled in. The lower hand should be drawn to point to the time when the awakenings will be discontinued. For the child in this example, the normal bedtime is 8:30 P.M., so the awakenings will have been discontinued, according to our rule, one hour after that, which is 9:30 P.M. Accord-

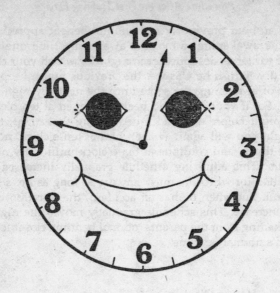

ingly, the hand in the illustration is drawn to point at 9:30. The other hand should be drawn to point to the parents' normal bedtime, which in this example is 12:30 A.M.

Each night that the child is dry, the time of awakening moves over one half hour and the space for that half-hour period should be shaded with the pencil. So, in the example shown, the child has been dry for three nights and is to be awakened at 11:00 P.M. The area between 11:00 P.M. and 12:30 A.M. is shaded in. If that child is again dry that night, the area from 10:30 to 11:00 P.M. will be shaded in to show that awakening will occur at 10:30. This representation allows the younger children to see their progress at a glance. When the space between the two hands is entirely filled, the awakenings will be discontinued, and this fact can be pointed out to the children at each bedtime. Each morning after a dry night, have your young child shade in the new area. By having your child do it, you are assuring your child's awareness of the progress being made. Using a colored crayon will make the progress still more evident as the area in color grows progressively larger. This method of representation is especially useful for children who have not yet mastered time-telling, but is also very useful for somewhat older children as a more vivid indication of progress than would be the case by simply writing down the scheduled hour of awakening.

In this example, the clock shows that the parents' bedtime is 12:30 A.M., that the child will be awakened at 11:00 P.M. the next night, and that the awakenings will be discontinued when the shaded area reaches 9:30 P.M.

Changing Sheets and Clothing

Your child will continue to be required to change his clothing and to remake the bed whenever he has had an accident. The procedure he is to follow has been described in the previous chapter for the intensive training day. He is to take off his wet nightclothes, put them in the designated dirty laundry container, obtain clean clothing, and dress himself. He is then to remove the wet sheets, also put them in the dirty laundry, obtain fresh sheets, and remake the bed as it was before the accident. This correction should be done as soon as you have detected the accident, which would normally be at the once-a-night awakening, or at the early-morning inspection one half hour before his normal awakening. Do not change his clothes or remake the bed yourself even though you could certainly do it more quickly. The pur-

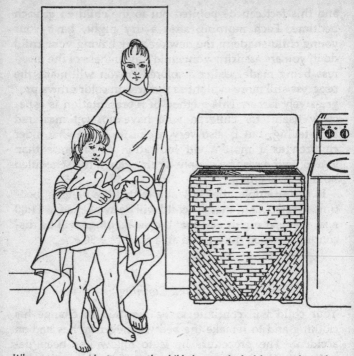

Whenever an accident occurs, the child changes the bedsheets and remakes the bed on his own.

pose of this procedure is to have your child take personal responsibility for his accident and its correction, and this can only come about if he does it all by himself.

Children are quite willing, and usually pleased, to take on this responsibility providing that they have been shown how to do it and if the requirement is communicated without anger. If the accident has been detected at the nightly awakening, your child may be reluctant to remake the bed because he is not fully awake. By gradually awakening him, and explaining the need for correction, he will usually do so quite readily. It is preferable to spend a few minutes awakening the child than to rush him before he is fully awake and perhaps irritable. The first few times he remakes the bed you should stand by to assure that he is doing it in the correct manner, but once having assured yourself, you should ask him to call you when he is finished. Changing the bed is now his responsibility, and you will be able to be more objective about his problem now that this chore is removed from you.

If the wet bed was not detected early enough in the morning, your child may not have enough time to remake the bed without being late for school, if he is of school age. In such circumstances leave the bed unmade until he returns from school.

Keep the clean bed sheets in a location easily accessible to the very young child, so that he can obtain them without your assistance.

Getting-up Practice

The getting-up practice was described briefly in the previous chapter concerning the intensive training day. Your child should have performed this practice before going to bed on that training night. The getting-up procedure will be performed from now on whenever your child has an accident. On the first training night, your child performed the getting-up practice simply as a demonstration of his ability to do the procedure even though he may not have had an accident. But now he will practice getting up whenever he has an accident. If the accident is detected at the morning inspection, he will do the practice at that time as well as that night before he goes to bed. If the

Whenever bedwetting has occurred, the next night the child does twenty trials of the getting-up practice, in which he rushes to the bathroom after imagining that he is asleep and had the urge to urinate.

accident was detected at the nightly awakening, he will do the practicing at the time he was awakened and again before he goes to bed the next night. The purpose of the getting-up practice, you will recall, is to establish the act of arising from bed as a very strong habit so that your child will be able to do so automatically at night, even when he is sound asleep, whenever he has the need to urinate. If he has no accident, then he has learned how to handle the problem and there is no need for him to have to practice. But, whenever he has an accident, this indi-cates that he has not yet learned to get up easily in response to his bladder signals and needs more practice in doing so. By arranging for the practice only when accidents have occurred, it will be done only when it is needed.

The reason that the practicing is done at the two scheduled times is to associate the act of getting up closely in time with the bedwetting. For the practice to be most effective, it should be done under circumstances that resemble most closely those existing during sleep. In the morning when the child is awakened after an accident, he is still sleepy, so the situation is fairly similar to the situation during actual sleep, and practicing at that time can be expected to be more effective than at other times when he is fully awake. The second practice period is given at bedtime, even though the child is fairly awake at that time, since the child can be expected to remember best during his sleep those actions that took place immediately before falling asleep. As with the morning practice period, this bedtime practice is closely associated in time with the sleep period and can be expected to be more effective for that reason as well.

The getting-up practice, you will recall, consisted of the child lying down in bed for about one minute while pretending to be asleep, and then arising quickly to rush to the bathroom where he briefly tried to urinate. He then returned to the bed and repeated this sequence for a total of twenty trials. To make this practice most effective, try to arrange the situation so that it is as similar as possible to the situation that exists during actual sleep. Have the lights dimmed or shut off just as they normally are at night. Have your child close his eyes as they will be during actual sleep. Have him breathe slowly and deeply and lie in the posture that he usually adopts when asleep, such as curling up on his side. Tell him to relax his body and to pretend that he is sleeping.

To provide sufficient time to create the sensations of sleep, the child should lie in bed for about one minute. This duration need not be exact and should not be timed. However, to give the younger child an approximate idea of what a one-minute duration is, you should have him count slowly to fifty or to recite the alphabet slowly during the first few trials as he rests in bed. If the interval seems much too short, have him recite aloud at first so that you can show him how to recite more slowly. But, discontinue this recitation as soon as your child has learned to approximate a one-minute duration, since that is not a natural thought sequence during sleep.

During this pretended sleep, we wish to have the child concentrate on his bladder sensations. When he is very relaxed, tell him to think about the feelings in his stomach and whether it feels as if he has to go to the toilet. Tell him to strain slightly, and when he feels as if he has to go even just a little bit, have him quickly jump out of bed and rush to the bathroom. If he does not have any feeling whatsoever that he has to urinate, then tell him to pretend that he has to go by thinking what it has felt like in the past. As he lies in bed, softly instruct him to direct his thoughts to this imagined need to urinate. For example, you might say, "Larry, remember to jump up just as soon as you feel like you have to go. Think about how it feels when you have to go. Think hard. . . ." If you have the time to remain with your child throughout the twenty practice trials, you should do so to assure that he is performing them correctly, and you can continue to prompt your child on several of the trials to direct his thoughts to his need to urinate. But, if your time is limited, then try to be present during at least the first one or two trials to assure that he has started off correctly. When he is performing the rest of the trials on his own while you are doing something else, have him call out from the bathroom which practice trial he has just completed so that you can follow his progress at a distance.

The getting-up practice is probably the single most important procedure in this training program. The procedure teaches the child to be aware of his bladder sensations while asleep, and teaches him a positive alternative response that will prevent wetting. It is true that the procedure requires about one half hour of the child's time and at least a few minutes of the parent's time for each practice period, but it will be recalled that the results of the studies showed that the average child required this practice on only four days before two consecutive weeks of dryness occurred, since the average child had only four accidents before achieving that goal. Consequently, this procedure should be carried out very conscientiously on the few occasions when it is needed. The child should be given a thorough explanation of the need for the procedure: It is a skill that must be overlearned since it must be carried out when he is asleep. Under no circumstances is the procedure to be presented to the child as a punishment for wetting, but rather as something constructive that he can do to prevent wetting. Should your child begin to show reluctance to perform the procedure, repeat your explanation of why the procedure is needed. To encourage him, spend as much time with him as he practices as you can conveniently spare and praise him for his efforts.

The getting-up practice is to be carried out after the child has remade his bed after an accident, and then again the next night before bedtime. The sequence, then, is that when a wetting has been detected, the child first remakes his bed and then does the getting-up practice. The next night, he again does the practice at bedtime. Each acci-

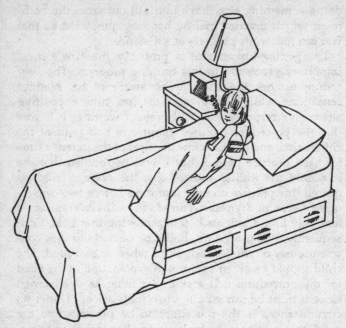

Before going to bed each night, the child feels the sheets to make him aware of their dry feeling and he rehearses what he will do if he has the need to urinate.

dent therefore results in two separate half-hour periods of getting-up practice, one period being spent right after the accident and the other being spent at the next bedtime.

Early Bedtime Practice in Getting Up

If your child had an accident the night before, he should practice the getting-up procedure before going to bed the next night. Since this practice will take about a half hour, the normal bedtime would be delayed unless he started earlier. Accordingly, have your child do the getting-up practice one half hour before his normal bedtime if he had a bedwetting the night before. Explain beforehand to your child that people remember during their sleep, such as in dreams, those thoughts they had right before going to sleep and that is why the getting-up practice is needed right before he goes to bed. Some children complain that the practice keeps them from some other activity, such as playing or television viewing. Explain to him that his bedtime would be delayed unless the practice is started earlier.

Bedtime Reminders

When your child goes to bed at night, you will perform several procedures designed to help focus his attention on the need to stay dry. Several of these procedures were also used at the end of the intensive training day. You will continue to use them now every night at bedtime.

AWARENESS OF BED SHEETS

When your child is asleep, he will only have a dim awareness that his bed is wet. To increase this awareness, you will have him touch and stroke the bed sheet to "feel its dryness," and to concentrate on how it feels. Ask him to close his eyes momentarily as he runs his hands along the sheet and to tell you whether he can remember this dry feeling.

BEDTIME REMINDER OF HOW TO DEAL WITH URGE TO URINATE

At bedtime, you want to be reassured that your child remembers what he is to do if he has the urge to urinate. Simply telling him not to wet the bed is a negative statement which does not tell him what positive actions he should take. The positive action which he can take, of course, is to arise quickly from the bed and hurry to the bathroom. The other positive action is to hold back just as he had done so successfully on the intensive training day. As he goes to sleep, you want to be sure he remembers these two reactions and is carrying these thoughts into his sleep. Ask him what he will do when he has the urge, rather than telling him, so that you can tell from his answer that he really does know. If he gives a partial answer, such as, "I'll hold it back until I don't have to go anymore," then ask him what else he must do, rather than you providing the missing information. In response to the above partial answer, you might ask, "And what else should you do? Run to the toilet? That's right. I'm sure you can do it. Are you thinking hard about how you will do it? Good, that will help you remember when you're asleep."

BEDTIME AWARENESS OF "FULL FEELING"

You also want your child to be very aware of his bladder sensations and any urge to urinate at this crucial moment before falling asleep so that he will also carry that thought with him into sleep. To help him have this awareness, have him describe how his stomach feels as he is lying down in bed and ask if he feels any need to urinate. "Do you feel you have to go at all?" If he does, ask him what he should do. "Jump up and go to the toilet." Tell him to do so. If he says he has no need, ask him to strain to try to create the urge. If he can, then again ask him what he should do, and have him go to the bathroom, reminding him to do the same thing at night.

BEDTIME REVIEW OF PROGRESS

You do not wish your child to fall asleep with fear and doubts in his mind. Accordingly, do not threaten or warn. Such threats are to be avoided at any time and bedtime is especially important. Instead, concentrate on his positive achievements and review them at this time so that he will fall asleep feeling proud of himself and assured that he will once again be successful. Remind him of his previous dry nights. "I know you can do it again; you've been dry for four nights in a row." Even if he had an accident recently, stress the positive, such as by saying, "You've been dry for four nights out of the last seven, looking at your Progress Calendar. That's fantastic! Before we started you couldn't do it at all. At this rate, you'll be dry almost every night. I know you can do it." Even if this is the first day after the intensive training day, you can stress the positive by reviewing his achievement on the intensive training day. "Yesterday, you were dry all night, even with all of that drinking. That's amazing. That shows you can control yourself now, and I'm proud of how well you did! Let's make it another dry night." Also, as part of this progress review, comment on his success in increasing his bladder control by the holding-back practice. "Today you filled the cup to at least six ounces every time. That's more than ever, so I know you can hold it back now. You sure are learning fast in solving this problem." In addition, you can point out his progress

Each morning, one half hour before the child normally wakes up, the bed is inspected for wetness. If it is wet, the child changes the sheets at that time and does the getting-up practice.

in the getting-up practice and tell him how that is becoming a well-practiced habit.

Morning Inspection

If you have not used the buzzer apparatus, you will not have known whether a bedwetting occurred until the morning. Since we wish your child to remake the bed if it is wet, allow enough time for him to do so by inspecting the bed one half hour before the normal time for getting up. If the bed sheets are felt to be dry, allow your child to continue sleeping for the additional half hour. But if by touching the sheets, the bed is found to be wet, awaken your child immediately so that the next half hour can be spent in changing the sheets and in practicing the getting-up trials.

If you have used the buzzer apparatus, then these early-morning inspections theoretically are not necessary, since any bedwetting will have been signaled during the night at the moment that wetting occurred and your child would have already changed his clothes and the sheets. Nevertheless, the buzzer apparatus does not always operate properly so it is possible that wetting has occurred but the buzzer did not sound. It is advisable, therefore, to check your child's sheets for wetness a half hour before your child's normal wake-up time even if the buzzer was used.

What If You Do Use the Pad-and-Buzzer Apparatus?

The method has been described up to now under the assumption that you have decided not to use the buzzer apparatus. Some slight changes will occur if you do decide to use it.

The principal difference in the procedure when using the apparatus is that the changing of the bed sheets and the getting-up practice are done when the buzzer sounds rather than when you inspect the bed. The pad-and-buzzer apparatus provides constant inspection and a loud signal when bedwetting occurs. Otherwise, the inspections are made only in the morning and at the scheduled nightly awakening. So, if the buzzer sounds at 3:00 A.M., then you will arise, awaken your child, have him change

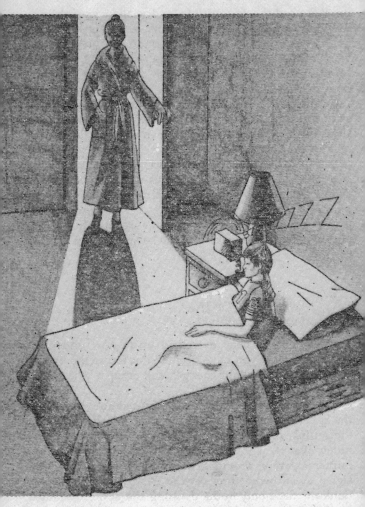

The pad-and-buzzer apparatus makes learning faster by giving an immediate signal when the bed is wet. It is inconvenient because it wakes everybody up in the middle of the night.

the sheets, and engage in the getting-up practice before he returns to bed. In the infrequent event that two bed-wettings occur during one night, you should have your child remake the bed and perform the getting-up practice after each wetting. The apparatus is reset by you after a wetting so it is capable of detecting a second wetting that might occur that night.

Because wettings are detected automatically, there is theoretically no need to inspect the bed for wetting, either at the nightly awakening or early in the morning. But, no apparatus is foolproof, and some bedwettings do fail to activate the apparatus. Perhaps the apparatus was not plugged in, or the pad is in the wrong position, or the apparatus is internally defective, or the child unplugged it. Or, the buzzer may have sounded but the child then disconnected it and went back to sleep before you noticed it. All of these possibilities are relatively rare, but they do occur and will slow down the learning. Therefore, as an extra precaution, check the bed for wetness at the nightly awakening and also in the morning even though the apparatus theoretically should make these inspections unnecessary.

The apparatus manufacturers usually supply detailed instructions for the proper use of the apparatus, and these directions should, of course, be followed. A few aspects of the proper use should be stressed. First, the child should be given a thorough explanation of the purpose of the apparatus and its operation. A trial demonstration beforehand is useful during the day in which you pour some water on the pad so that he can know what the buzzer sounds like. Also, it is advisable to have the child sleep without nightclothes below the waist so that the urine will flow freely onto the pad and not be absorbed in large part by the nightclothes. Before bedtime, and again at the scheduled nightly awakening, check the apparatus for proper connection and position. When the buzzer sounds, try to arise as soon as possible to help the child awaken and supervise his cleaning up and his practice.

For some of the pad-and-buzzer apparatuses, one change can be made in the procedure which makes its usage more economical. These apparatuses usually consist of a sandwich-like arrangement in which a large sheet of absorbent paper is inserted between an upper and lower metal sheet. The upper metal sheet is porous to allow urine to flow through it into the absorbent sheet of paper. When this paper becomes wet, the buzzer sounds. When the apparatus is purchased, several sheets of paper are enclosed, since they must be replaced after each wetting; more sheets of paper must be purchased for continued use of the apparatus. To reduce this expense and inconvenience, absorbent cloth may be used instead of the absorbent paper. An ordinary cloth bed sheet can be cut into several small sections, each of them being the same size as and used instead of the sheet of paper. Since the cloth sheets are reusable after being washed and dried, additional paper sheets need not be purchased. Parents have generally preferred to use the cloth sheets, especially if the bedwetting of their child persists for a longer time than is usual. Since this substitute of cloth sheets may not be possible with all types of pad-and-buzzer apparatuses, it is suggested that the new arrangement be tested beforehand by dripping water on the pad.

Calendar Progress Chart

Each morning at wake-up time, have your child mark the Dry-Bed Calendar which is posted next to the bed. If the bed was dry that night, mark it as "D" for dry or simply

DRY-BED CALENDAR

MON	TUES	WED	THURS	FRI	SAT	SUN
	1	2	3	4	5	6
7	8	9 *Dry*	10 *Dry*	11 *Wet*	12 *Dry*	13 *Dry*
14 *Dry*	15 *Wet*	16 *Dry*	17 *Dry*	18 *Dry*	19 *Dry*	20 *Dry*
21 *Dry*	22 *Dry*	23 *Dry*	24 *Dry*	25 *Dry*	26 *Dry*	27 *Dry*
28 *Dry*	29	30	31			

write "Dry," using large letters. Or if the bed was wet, mark it "W" for wet or simply "Wet." A sample filled-in Dry-Bed Calendar is shown in the illustration. In that example, the child was wet on the third night, Friday, then had three dry nights before the next accident on the following Tuesday, after which he was dry for the next thirteen nights. Blank forms that can be used for this calendar are printed on separate pages in Appendix 7, and they can be torn out and used if you do not have a separate calendar. The blank calendars have the days of the week listed, such as Sunday, Monday, and so forth, but not the dates, such as Oct. 1, 2, 3, and so forth, since they differ for each month, so fill in the numbers for the month in which you are starting. Continue to record on the Dry-Bed Calendar until at least one month has passed without an accident. At wake-up time and at bedtime have your child look at the Dry-Bed Calendar and you make some comments about the progress being shown, praising him for it. This calendar will enable you and your child to determine at a glance when he can receive the benefits you had agreed upon after different numbers of dry nights, such as having his brother sleep with him after four dry nights. Also, when you wish to inform any of your friends or his friends of his progress you can do so easily by showing them the Dry-Bed Calendar. Even when an occasional accident occurs, the calendar shows how minor the accident is in the long-term view.

Keeping the Agreement of Benefits

Before training started, you made an agreement with your child as to several benefits that you would provide as he achieved dryness. You should now enthusiastically pro-

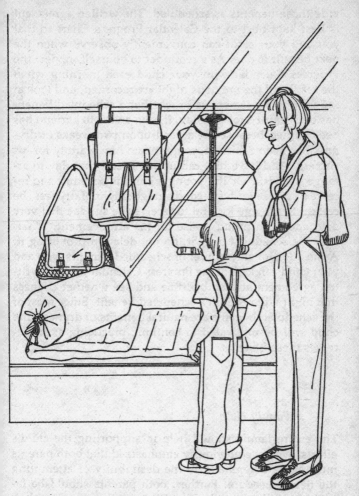

When the child starts staying dry at night, give him the promised rewards,
such as the sleeping bag and overnight trips.

vide those benefits as scheduled. The written agreement is best kept next to the Calendar Progress Chart so that you and your child can conveniently observe when the next benefit is due. As a reminder to yourself, review the Progress Calendar with your child each morning when the results of the previous night are recorded, and look at the written agreement as to whether a scheduled benefit has been earned for that day. If, say, a visit to a friend has been earned because the agreed-upon two weeks of dryness has been achieved, congratulate him warmly for his success. And have him call up his friend that day to arrange the visit. Or if a younger child is scheduled to receive a sundae for his second straight night of dryness, be certain to arrange for him to receive the sundae that very day, and with proud praise for his achievement. Whatever the scheduled benefit, do not delay in providing it. As an additional reminder of scheduled benefits, you and your child can look at the Progress Calendar and the written agreement at each bedtime and see whether dryness that night will result in a scheduled benefit. Since most of the scheduled benefits are natural benefits of dryness, the child will be motivated to continue practicing as he receives these benefits.

Family Help

The entire family should help in supporting the child's efforts. We have previously emphasized that both parents must agree beforehand to the desirability of attempting the new procedure. Further, both parents should be familiar with the procedure so that one can supervise when the other is too busy or away. The child will make more of an effort when he sees that both parents are involved

The child should receive encourgement from both parents and other members of the family for his progress in staying dry.

and will not fall into the pattern sometimes seen in other areas of playing one parent off against the other.

If there are other children in the family, they, too, should be informed of the reasons for the various procedures in this training program so that they will understand why the child is doing these things. Ask the other children to help the child by telling him to keep trying. Show them the Happy-Face Clock and the Progress Calendar and the progress being made. If they are not actively encouraged to praise the child, then, instead, they may tease or criticize. One of the rewards for the younger child may be to sleep with a brother or sister, and this should be encouraged to promote their mutual involvement.

At breakfast each morning, the parents should comment on whether the child has been dry and if so, prompt the other children to praise the child for his success. Even if an accident occurred, comment on his having cleaned up, practiced, and on the successes he has had previously.

At supper, again the parents should mention their confidence that the child will be dry that night and, similarly, prompt the other children to do the same.

In combination, this praise and reassurance from the entire family will create an enthusiasm about practicing and maintaining awareness of his urinary habits.

Telling Friends and Relatives

Bedwetting is a problem which is generally known only to family members; usually only one or two other persons may know about it, such as a grandmother, aunt, babysitter, or next-door neighbor. The very young child often places great importance on the approval of these persons. If so, the child will be motivated by informing them of his successes, and this provision should be considered for inclusion in the benefits agreement. Call these persons on the phone and have them speak to the child, expressing their pleasure at the progress being achieved. If one of these persons visits the house, have him or her look at the Progress Calendar and tell the child how well he is doing. Older children are likely to feel ashamed to discuss the problem with others, but young children are usually encouraged by this support from outside the immediate household family.

Rewards for Younger Children

In addition to your enthusiastic praise you should also give rewards to young children, since such rewards carry

Show your pride in your child by encouraging him for every small indication of progress.

more of a meaning for them that you really do approve. So, for young children, give them a small piece of candy, a favorite drink, a trip to the shopping center, a ride, or whatever else you know the child likes very much, and do this whenever you praise. The size or amount of the reward can be very small since the important feature is that the reward is a visible and concrete indication of approval. For example, you might say, "Thelma, you filled the glass way up this time, twelve ounces! Come with me, I'm going to give you a potato chip." Or "You had two dry nights, Walter; let's celebrate by having a picnic today."

Positive Attitude Toward Your Child's Efforts

Throughout training try to maintain a positive attitude toward all of your child's efforts even when your child is not doing as well as he might seem to be able to do. Your child will be trying to control an action in his sleep, a task which is a great challenge whatever the action might be. This program teaches the skills of bladder control, bladder awareness, rapid awakening, and toileting, but in addition your child will require great motivation to persist in his efforts in spite of an occasional accident at first. Praise your child for everything he does in connection with his training. Praise your child throughout the holding-back trials on the first day, such as, "Wanda, you waited the whole two minutes. That's a long time," or, "Sammy, you held back for the whole two minutes on the bed. You should do very well tonight, too." Praise your child for getting up by himself when the buzzer sounds. "Allen, I'm so pleased you got up to change even before I got here. I'm glad you're taking care of things by yourself."

And, of course, every night without an accident should result in praise. "You did it, Betty! You went the whole night without wetting! That's the first time and I am so proud of you." Or, "Carl, imagine that, two nights in a row with no accidents! I think you licked the problem with your trying so hard."

What If My Child Has a Temper Tantrum and Won't Practice?

Occasionally, a child becomes upset after an accident and refuses to change his sheets or do the getting-up practice and may even have a temper tantrum. This refusal is more likely to occur at night when the child was awakened by the sounding of the buzzer after an accident or at one of the scheduled awakenings. The child is sleepy and one can sympathize with his reluctance.

The child is less likely to refuse to change the sheets or practice getting up by your being certain before the training starts that the child fully understands why these activities must be carried out. The nightclothes and the sheets were wet by him, not by the parent, so he should change them. That when he changes them, rather than the parent, the parent will not get annoyed. That they must be changed right away so that the bed will be a clean place to sleep in, and he will not get a skin rash, and he won't get used to sleeping in a wet bed. The getting-up practice must be done in order to get into the habit of getting up in his sleep when he is wet. That it wasn't learned well enough; otherwise the accident wouldn't have occurred. That it must be done for twenty trials, rather than just one, because it isn't enough to know what to do, but to have it become a habit so he will do it even when asleep. Explain that you want him to be proud of himself when he has a dry bed and to know that it happened because of how hard he tried. These explanations should be given before the first training day and discussed until the child understands the reason for them in every way. Ask him if he agrees to do these things and provide additional discussion until he does agree.

Refusals will also be minimized by repeating the explanations at every opportunity as to why the changing of sheets and getting-up practice are needed. During the first training day when he does these activities without having had an accident, repeat the reasons. "Wilma, you made the bed all by yourself. Now Mommy won't get so mad, because now you're taking care of it," or, "Charlie, you ran so fast to the toilet. That's good. I'm sure you'll get to the bathroom fast enough when you really have to go."

Whenever an accident occurs again, repeat the reasons to the child as to why he must change his sheets and do the practice trials. "David, you had an accident, but you changed the sheets so now you won't get a rash or get used to sleeping in a wet bed." Or, "Evelyn, you did the whole twenty practices by yourself. I'm proud. Now you know how to get up much better than you did before this accident."

If the child has a tantrum, or refuses to change sheets or practice in spite of the prior explanations and agreements, do not become angry. Instead calm him down first. Perhaps he is not fully awake so talk to him for a few minutes, reassuring him of your love for him and telling him you'll talk to him about the reasons for doing the corrections until he has awakened and feels better. Have him sit on the toilet or a chair until he is calmed down and is willing to continue. It is important that the sheet changes and practice be done, but reassure him until he is calmed, and wait a few minutes until he is ready. He will realize that you are not punishing him, that you are sympathetic with the inconvenience involved for him, and that you will wait as long as is necessary, but he must start eventually.

While the child is sitting in a chair to "think about it" and to calm down, remove any distractions such as watching TV or playing or reading. He should concentrate on the need for practicing.

If the refusal occurs in the morning when the child is scheduled to leave for school, do not allow him to be late. Instead, have him do the cleaning up and practicing as soon as he returns from school.

To show your understanding, tell your child how sleepy he must be at being awakened at that hour, that you know it takes efforts to make the bed up, that you can understand how he gets tired getting up so many times to go to the toilet. By sympathizing with his annoyances, you are telling him you are looking at the situation just as he is and are not blaming him for his reluctance.

When he eventually does start to change the sheets or practice, you should immediately praise him for making the effort and remind him once again of how his efforts will prevent future accidents and will make him proud of himself.

What If My Child Wets When He Is Not Feeling Well?

We have already mentioned that training should not be started if your child is not feeling well. What should you do later when your child has been dry for many weeks but then becomes ill and starts wetting? These circumstances occur occasionally. When young children become ill, bedwetting sometimes starts again. If your child is too ill to make the bed himself or do the getting-up practice, you should not require him to do so. Yet, he may ask to be excused from the agreed-upon changing of the bed and practicing even though he feels only minimally ill and can easily do those things. A good general rule to follow if your child is going to school is that if he is too sick to attend school that day and must remain in bed, he should also be excused from cleaning up and practicing. Similarly, if your child is a preschooler, and is too ill to play outside or be involved in his usual activities, he also should be excused from cleaning up and practicing. Of course, if your doctor says his condition does not permit these activities, also excuse him. As soon as your child is able to go to school or resume his usual play activities or the doctor gives his permission, have your child clean up and practice after each accident once again.

8 | Ending the Training

Ending the Training

The present training program was designed to be effective in a short period of time and proved to be so when the various procedures were conscientiously and consistently carried out. The question, then, is when to end the training. When your child has remained dry for the first night, you may understandably feel that he has learned how to control the problem and that the training procedures are no longer needed. The evidence shows, however, that many nights of dryness must pass before we can be assured that the problem is solved. Your child is learning a new and difficult skill, and one night of dryness does not mean that he has reversed years of wetting. How many dry nights must pass?

When two weeks, that is fourteen consecutive days of dryness, have occurred, the chances are very good that your child has acquired nighttime control. The statistics show that most children will stay dry once they achieve fourteen straight dry nights. The others will have a brief return of bedwetting, but as we will discuss later, they will quickly become dry again when some of the procedures are temporarily reintroduced. So about two weeks of dryness is the cutoff duration that you will use in ending most of the procedures.

After two weeks of uninterrupted dryness, discontinue the pad-and-buzzer apparatus if you have been using it.

After two weeks of uninterrupted dryness, discontinue the bladder-control procedure. Your child no longer need urinate in the measuring cup. Encourage him to continue to hold back his urine as long as he can, but have him do so on his own.

After two weeks of uninterrupted dryness, you can discontinue the early-morning inspections of the bed. You no longer need to examine the bed for wetness one half hour before your child's normal time of arising. You should, however, continue to examine it at some time after he has awakened in the morning when it is convenient for you, just to be certain.

The nightly awakenings are discontinued according to the Happy Clock procedure already described. You will recall that your child is awakened one half hour earlier after each dry night. When the awakening was scheduled to occur within one hour of the normal bedtime, you discontinued it entirely. Your child will now sleep through the entire night without being awakened by you to toilet himself.

The continual praise and rewards for dryness are gradually decreased and, again, by the end of two weeks of uninterrupted dryness, are eliminated entirely as a formal procedure. Occasional spontaneous compliments are, however, natural and desirable.

The Progress Calendar Chart should continue to be

used until one month (thirty days) of uninterrupted dryness has elapsed. This procedure takes but a few seconds. You will continue to check the bed each morning. By having your child mark the chart each day with you, he will be reminded of your continued concern that he should try to stay dry.

The requirement that your child change the sheets should be permanent. Your child now understands that correcting the wetness is his responsibility and that he is responsible for remaking the bed if an occasional accident should ever happen again.

Similarly, the getting-up practice should be a permanent requirement. If an accident occurs after several weeks or months of dryness, that indicates that more practice is needed before going to bed that night.

The two permanent procedures are, therefore, the remaking of the bed and the getting-up practice. Since accidents will now rarely, if ever, occur, these two activities will be correspondingly infrequent since they are necessary only if an accident occurs.

What If Wettings Start Again?

For about one-fourth of the children, wetting may start again even though the child had been dry for several weeks or months before that. When such a wetting occurs, have your child change his clothes and the bed in the usual manner by himself and do the getting-up practice. As soon as the accident is discovered in the morning, have him change the bed sheets in the usual way and remind him of the need to practice that evening. A half hour before bedtime, have him do the getting-up practice for twenty trials and, at bedtime, have him feel the sheets and remind him of the need to stay dry, assuring him of your confidence in his ability to do so. Check the bed a half hour earlier the next morning so that if it is wet, time will be available for changing the sheets. Continue checking for a few days until no further wetting occurs. This simple and brief renewal of the getting-up practice and the bed changing should prevent further bedwettings. So when a bedwetting occurs after you thought they had been eliminated, treat the situation in a calm, problem-solving manner. On the one hand, do not ignore it and hope that it will not appear again. On the other hand, do not become angry with your child, nor assume that the bedwetting problem is as great as ever. Rather, consider the bedwetting as a signal that a little more practice is needed and that if the practice is carried out at the very first accident, no further accidents are likely to occur for a very long time.

9 | Some General Questions About Bedwetting Training

What Should I Do if the Procedure Does Not Work?

The results obtained in the studies with this method showed that all of the children who continued using the procedures stopped wetting their beds. So you should be strongly assured that your child, too, will be successful if the procedure is carried out in the same manner. But, we should realize that every child is different and that there is probably a very small number of children with whom the procedure might not be effective. Also, a misunderstanding may occur as to how to do the present training. If benefits are not seen within the first week, read over the description of the procedures once again to discover any such misunderstanding. If this review does not lead to successful training, consult a behavior therapist since they are the persons who are most likely to be familiar with this new method and can clarify misunderstandings or try to adapt the procedure to some special needs of your child. A list of some behavior therapists may be obtained from:

Association for Advancement of Behavior Therapy
420 Lexington Avenue
New York, New York 10017

Or you may prefer to seek professional help from a psychologist, medical doctor, or pediatrician.

Should I Try to Rely Only on This Book?

This book describes a program that has been successful when it was carried out by parents who, along with their child, were given an explanation of the procedure by a counselor. In addition, the counselor asked and answered questions and had the parent and child act out some of the procedures. This book is intended to be a partial substitute for a counselor in that it relies on a written explanation rather than spoken instructions and demonstrations. The extent to which you will be successful depends greatly on how well you understand and follow the instructions here. The best teacher of any new skill is someone who has had successful experience in teaching that skill previously, and the same is true of teaching a child to control his bladder at night. You might well make an effort, therefore, to obtain the assistance and advice of any other parents you know who have used this method successfully with their own child, or a professional behavior therapist, counselor, psychologist, doctor, or pediatrician who can explain the method and answer questions. Their instructions, plus the information you have obtained from this book, will make you better prepared to proceed.

Which Children Have More Difficulty Learning?

We might expect large differences in the ease of training children to stop bedwetting because of differences in age, in sex, in the prior frequency of bedwetting, and so forth. Surprisingly, studies have found little difference caused by most of these factors. Boys seem to learn at about the same rate as girls. Younger children, from three to six years, do learn more slowly than the older children of twelve to fourteen years, but the difference is fairly slight. Children who had wet every night learn about as fast as those who were wetting on only some of the nights. Similarly, not much difference is found between children with a high IQ and those with a low IQ, except perhaps when the IQ is so low as to indicate substantial mental retardation. One factor that seems to be important is whether the child has mastered toileting during the day. Those children who are still having daytime accidents require more training than those who are no longer having accidents. Consequently, the present procedure stresses that the child first be thoroughly trained in his daytime toileting. One might expect that bedwetting is associated with deep sleep, but this has not been found to be the case. What is important is whether the child learns to awaken to go to the bathroom. Children who do awaken to go to the toilet are more successful. For this reason, the present method emphasized teaching the child to awaken to toilet himself in response to his full bladder sensations.

Is Bedwetting a Sign of a Personality Disorder?

As embarrassing and troublesome as bedwetting is, one may wonder whether bedwetting is a signal of an underlying emotional disturbance or personality disorder. It has been found that bedwetting occurs for children who are well-adjusted as well as for those who are emotionally upset. So, you should not conclude that your child's bedwetting is necessarily evidence that your child has unusual emotional problems. The bedwetting does often cause emotional problems. It has been found that when bedwetting has been cured, the child generally shows an improvement in his attitude and adjustment. Emotional adjustment is also related to bedwetting in a different way. For some children who have been dry at night for months or years, a sudden emotional shock, such as the death of a parent or family member, may result in a return of bedwetting. In such instances, the emotional upset does seem to cause the bedwetting, but training such as is described in the present program will correct this bedwetting in the same way as it corrected that which had been present from early childhood. So, if bedwetting suddenly occurs again after an emotional disturbance, deal with the problems separately. Give your child the reassurance and support necessary to reduce the emotional problem as you normally would. Simultaneously, reintroduce the training procedures for bedwetting just as you would have done had the bedwetting reappeared without any emotional disturbance causing it. Bedwetting is a problem that occurs with or without a state of emotional disturbance and seems to cause emotional upset as much as it is caused by emotional upset. Staying dry should be viewed as a skill to be learned rather than as a sign of a healthy or unhealthy personality.

Mental Retardation

If your child is mentally retarded, the present method may still be used if the retardation is fairly mild. In that case, you definitely should use the buzzer apparatus to help him develop sensitivity to his bladder signals. You should also use the snack rewards especially frequently since he will then understand better that he has done something well and that you approve. Because of the retardation he may have difficulty understanding what you desire when you ask him to strain at the toilet and to hold back, so this procedure on the first day should be omitted if he has difficulty in comprehending it. Also because of the retardation, he may be unable to count to himself in bed during the getting-up practice so you should then time the period (about one minute) yourself, and not ask him to do so.

If your child is profoundly or severely retarded, the present program requires extensive modification, but bedwetting training is still possible. As mentioned earlier, the present program of research began with teaching retarded persons. A separate book has been published which deals specifically with toilet training and bedwetting training of severely retarded persons and is listed in the References at the back of this book.

Reminder Outline and Questions

To assist you in remembering the various procedures, outlines are included in the various Appendixes.

In Appendix 1 there is a list of questions that serve as reminders of the preparations you make before starting training.

Appendix 2 is an outline of the training procedures to be used only during the intensive training day.

Appendix 3 outlines the procedures to be used regularly after the intensive training day, and Appendix 4 describes when each of the procedures should be discontinued. Each of these outlines is used at a different stage of training. By having these outlines before you, they will serve as a reminder of the procedures and the sequence in which they are to be used.

Appendix 8 is a self-test to help you determine how well you remember the procedures described in this book. It is recommended that you take this self-test after reading the book. If you have difficulty in answering some questions, you will benefit from reading again those sections of the book that deal with those questions. Also, the answers to the questions on the self-test are given on the page following the questions.

10 A Bedtime Story About a Boy Who Stopped Bedwetting

The following story about Timmy describes the common thoughts and actions of young bedwetters who have used this training procedure. The names are fictitious and the events do not describe one actual person's experiences, but are a composite of those of children who have been trained by our method.

Consider using this story to be read to your child at bedtime to help inform him about the training procedure. Of course, if your child is older and can read well, have him read this story himself or even, as was noted earlier, he might read the rest of the book as well. Your child should read the story or have it read to him a few days before you start the training so that he will know what to expect. As you read the story, feel free to interrupt to comment on how Timmy, the hero of this story, has had experiences similar to those of your child.

* * *

Timmy was eight years old and was in the third grade at school. Sandler was his last name, Timmy Sandler. His friends sometimes called him Sandy and he liked that nickname because it reminded him of the sandy beach where he always had so much fun.

Timmy smiled and laughed a lot so the other children liked to play with him because he was so much fun to be with. At school, the other children liked to play with him at recess. And when there was no school, the other boys often came by the house to ask him to play and to be on their team.

But Timmy had a problem that his friends didn't know about. He wet his bed at night.

Almost no one knew he wet his bed except, of course, his mother and his father and his big sister, Betty, and a few people who found out about it by accident, like when his sister told her friends one day. He found out because all of a sudden Betty's friends came over to him at school and began calling him terrible names like "Baby," "Pee-Baby," and "Water-Bucket."

And Betty wasn't always very nice about it, either. They liked to play together and Betty taught him many new things. But when they had a quarrel and Betty became angry, she started calling him "Baby," too. So now he was afraid to play with her anymore. Mom told Betty to stop teasing and never again to tell any of her friends about the bedwetting, that Timmy would stop soon by himself if people didn't nag him about it. Timmy was very glad to hear his mother say that. He didn't want anybody in the world to know.

Timmy's mother knew, of course. Every morning she would look at the bed and say, "Oh, no!" "Again?" or, "Won't this ever end?" or something like that. Then she would make up the bed and sound upset and talk about all the work and all the laundry she was doing and kept talking like that all the while that she was putting away the wet sheets and making the bed. When she acted like that, Timmy went to another room to hide so he wouldn't hear her. For the last few months, though, she didn't say anything except, "Don't worry Timmy, you'll outgrow it. Just keep trying." But you could tell she wasn't happy.

Timmy's father didn't say too much about it. In fact, he acted a little surprised when Timmy's mother told him not long ago that maybe the bedwetting would stop if Timmy had more blankets to keep him warm. "Is my big man still wetting?" he asked, and patted Timmy on the head, but didn't say anything else about the bedwetting or the blankets.

A few other grown-ups knew about the bedwetting. Uncle Jack and Auntie Susan knew because Timmy wet one of their beds when he was visiting them two years ago. Grandma knew because his mother asked her once for help and now she asked about it almost every time she called. Some of his mother's friends knew about it because his mother had once asked them at her bridge club and now they always asked him, "Have you stopped wetting yet?" when the bridge club met at his house.

But Timmy usually didn't answer when people asked him about it. He didn't want to talk about it and never told anybody, even if someone did ask.

What could he do about it? He was asleep when it happened. Sometimes he dreamed that he was going in the toilet, or behind a tree or a bush, but that was all he could remember. He thought about it a lot, but what did everybody expect him to do? "I can't help it, I try," he told his mother. "Please don't be mad at me."

Timmy and his mother had tried many different things. They went to the doctor who asked him many questions and said Timmy was very healthy and that there was nothing wrong with him, that he would outgrow it soon. That was a very long time ago.

Then they tried not drinking. No milk or Cokes at supper. And never any drinks after supper, even when they went out to eat or to the ice cream store. Timmy felt left out, although he hoped it would help. It didn't.

The hardest thing his mother did was wake him up every hour all night long for about two weeks. He didn't mind it so much after a while. He would do anything that would help, but his mother got very angry after the first few nights and complained about being sleepy all the time. A few times her alarm clock didn't wake her up and she didn't awaken Timmy and he wet his bed, so she gave up on that.

Then she told him to sleep on his back and went into the bedroom to turn him over if he wasn't. That didn't work either. So she had him sleep on his stomach for a few nights. Still, the wettings went on. Someone else said that a hard bed was good, so a hard board was put under the mattress. Still no change.

They went back to the doctor and he gave them some pills for Timmy to take. But the pills made him so sleepy that he had to stop taking them.

"I give up," his mother had said after the pills. Now she never said anything about wetting. She had heard that bedwetting might be happening because Timmy was unhappy. So she tried even harder to make him happy and never scolded him, especially about bedwetting.

One day his mother came home with another idea. She just heard from a friend in the bridge club about a way of stopping bedwetting that had worked for her friend's daughter who was only four years old. Mrs. Golden, her friend, had gone to a psychologist who showed Mr. and Mrs. Golden and their girl, Cindy, a new training program. He had them practice it in the office for about an hour and gave them some papers which described the procedure to take home with them. Cindy had started two weeks ago and had only two accidents since then. Mrs. Golden suggested that Timmy's mother try it, too, even though she had "given up." So Timmy's mother read the report and asked Mrs. Golden to tell her about the new method.

Mrs. Golden said that she did not believe it either, herself, at first, but decided to give it a try. She was told by the psychologist that the average child who used this method had only one or two wettings on the very first week and had only four wettings before being dry for two straight weeks. And sure enough, her girl Cindy did even better so far. The way she described it, Cindy was given exercises to help increase her bladder control so she wouldn't have to go to the bathroom so often. Cindy was taught to get up in her sleep automatically when she had to go, and she was taught how to concentrate on this at night and to get up quickly when she had to. One of the nicest things was that now Cindy made up the bed and her mother didn't have to. Mrs. Golden said many other things, but Timmy's mother had heard enough to know that she was going to try it.

She called the number Mrs. Golden gave her and made an appointment at a time when Timmy and her husband could come with her, since all three had to be there: Timmy, his mother, and his father. When they arrived, the psychologist, who was a woman, took Timmy into a room alone after she had talked to him and his parents and had given them some papers to fill out. She told Timmy that from now on he was in charge of stopping the bedwetting. She had him practice "holding back" when he had to go to the bathroom and also had him practice getting up quickly at night, using a sofa in the office as if it were Timmy's bed. She had Timmy practice feeling his bed sheets at night and thinking hard about how his tummy felt when he had to go to the toilet. Timmy answered questions about what he should do when he had an accident from now on. It all sounded so easy to Timmy that he was sure he could do it. Then she called Timmy's mother and father in and asked Timmy to explain to them what he was going to do and to ask them to help him.

Timmy told his mother and father that his mother wouldn't have to change the sheets anymore, that he would take care of it. And that he was going to do lots of practicing to stop from wetting. He would practice getting up over and over and over until he was able to get up even when he was asleep. And he would practice waiting when he had to go to the toilet so that he could wait at night, too. In the beginning, until he practiced enough, he would get up once each night to go to the toilet so he wouldn't have to hold back for so long. And every night at bedtime he would think real hard about whether he had to go to the toilet and about getting up if he had to.

Timmy also told his parents how they could help him. On the first day, which would be a very busy practicing day, they would give him lots of Cokes and nice drinks and remind him every half hour to practice holding back. Every night his parents would help him to think about getting up. He wanted his mother to teach him how to change the sheets and make up the bed. When he practiced his getting-up exercises, he would ask them to watch him so that they could know how hard he was practicing. He would like them to tell him nice things when they saw him practicing the right way. When he stayed dry, he hoped they would give him something that he couldn't have before because he was wetting. And they would talk to Betty, his sister, to stop teasing him and ask her to help him, too.

Timmy's mother and father were delighted at how well Timmy understood the new training idea and how excited he was at helping himself. They told Timmy that they would do all of these things for him and that they felt sure he would be a success because he was so excited about it.

Before Timmy and his parents left the office, they made some promises about what Timmy should get to do once he started being dry. This is what they decided.

AGREEMENT

A BIG MILK SHAKE

When Timmy has been *dry for one night,* Dad will take him the next day after dinner for the biggest milk shake the store has. (Timmy was afraid to drink before bedtime so this was something special he could do if he didn't have to worry about wetting.) And a sundae the next night, too, if he's dry.

TELL GRANDMA

When Timmy has been *dry for three nights* in a row, we will call Grandma and let you tell her how you have learned how to stop wetting.

PLASTIC SHEET

When Timmy has been *dry for five nights,* he can take the plastic sheet off his bed. (Timmy hated that plastic sheet because it reminded him that he was still wetting.)

PAJAMAS

When Timmy is *dry for six nights*, we'll go to the store and buy him nice new pajamas.

HAVE FRIEND OVER

When Timmy is *dry for seven nights*, he can call a friend —either Larry, Bill, or Dick—and have him sleep over the next Friday or Saturday night that we are at home.

SLEEPING BAG

When Timmy has been *dry for ten nights*, we'll buy him a sleeping bag the next time we go shopping that's less than $20.

VISITING RELATIVES OVERNIGHT

When Timmy has been *dry for twelve nights*, we'll call Auntie Susan and Uncle Jack and arrange for an overnight visit to their house in the country with the apple trees. (Remember, Timmy had wet one of their beds during his last visit there.)

CAMP

When Timmy has gone for *fifteen nights dry*, we'll send the money to the summer camp so he can go this summer.

In addition, according to the training plan, Timmy will not be awakened to toilet at night after he had had *six dry nights*.

And when *two weeks of straight dryness* with no accidents has passed, Timmy will not use the measuring cup anymore when he goes to the toilet.

After *one month of straight dryness*, Timmy will not use the Calendar Chart anymore and will not do the bedtime practice of feeling the sheets. And Mom and Dad will not check the bed each morning anymore.

Timmy's father wrote out the agreements. Before they left, the psychologist told Timmy to call every day to tell her how he did the night before and that she would be calling him, too, in case he had any questions. She gave Timmy's mother some pages to look at at home to help remind them of the things they were to do.

Mr. Sandler was eager to start. He hadn't realized how much Timmy really wanted to stay dry but just hadn't known what to do. He told Timmy's mother that he wanted to help in the training, too.

Timmy's mother had tried so many other ways before that she couldn't be sure anything would work until she actually saw it happen. But this training did seem different in so many ways. Instead of cutting out drinks, it gave more drinks. Instead of waking Timmy up every hour all night long for weeks, she only had to wake him up once each night, and always before she went to bed herself. And making Timmy's bladder bigger, that seemed like such a good idea. She remembered that he went to the toilet so often during the day, too, and couldn't wait once he had to go. As to practicing getting up at night, that made more sense than just telling him to get up or not to wet. She wondered why she hadn't thought of that herself. As for Timmy making his own bed, that part of it was worth the effort even if he never did stop wetting. Seeing is believing, she thought.

Timmy's thoughts were different. Now he could do something about wetting instead of being told over and over again to try. Try what? Now he could practice holding back so his bladder in his tummy could hold more. That made sense. And now he could practice getting up at night so he could do it automatically, like riding a bike, without having to think about it. And now he could practice thinking how his tummy felt when he had to go. That was like learning to pay attention to his stomach when it started "growling," and he learned that meant it was mealtime and he should hurry home so he wouldn't be late for dinner.

Timmy and his mother and father talked on the way home about when they should start. Timmy wanted to start tomorrow, which was Friday. Dad wanted to start Saturday when he could help. But Timmy was so eager, they decided to start the next day right after Timmy came home from school. Dad would help when he came home from work at 5:30.

Mrs. Sandler looked at the reminder list she had been given as soon as they came home. She went over it with Timmy.

The first question on the reminder list was whether Timmy was old enough. Yes, he was over three years old.

Had Timmy stopped pants-wetting during the day? Yes, about five years ago. Yes, he had been given a medical exam already. But, what about the drinks and snacks? Timmy helped her get the soda, the kind without sugar, and some potato chips.

Was there a light in the hall and a night-light in the bedroom? They checked, and the one in the bedroom had burned out so they replaced it. Was his bed in a convenient location? They decided to move it away from the wall so he could make it up more easily, and closer to the bedroom door so he could get to the bathroom faster. Have the other children been informed? His sister, Betty, was all full of questions when they had come home, and they told her what Timmy was going to do.

What about the pad-and-buzzer apparatus? Mr. Sandler didn't like that idea and neither did Mrs. Sandler because they didn't want to get up in the middle of the night. Timmy didn't like the idea of a gadget in his bed. But they all agreed that if the buzzer was needed, they wouldn't mind too much if it helped. They decided to wait one week. If the wetting didn't stop at all, they would use it. Mrs. Sandler remembered seeing them for sale in mail-order catalogs and other places.

What about a measuring cup for Timmy to use when he went to the toilet? Mrs. Sandler had a Pyrex measuring cup that was big enough. It held 16 ounces and had the numbers marked on the side. Timmy got a note pad and put it in the bathroom with a pencil for writing down the numbers.

The next thing was a calendar for marking whether Timmy was wet or dry each night. Betty said she had a calendar in her room they could have. Everyone thanked her for being so helpful.

The next reminder was to choose a day to start training. Now that they had everything, they decided for sure to start tomorrow. Timmy would come home from school as early as he could so he could start right away. And tonight he would go to sleep early since he would be waking up a lot tomorrow on the first day of training.

Had both parents agreed on a training plan? Mrs. Sandler checked with Mr. Sandler. They both thought all of the procedures made sense. The next question was whether Timmy's pajamas were loose enough. They checked and realized that Timmy had grown a lot. The pajamas were very tight. Betty offered to let him use her pajamas, which she had outgrown, until he got new ones.

Had a written agreement been made about special treats for staying dry? Yes, they had done that at the psychologist's office. Dad got some thumbtacks and put the agreement on the wall next to Timmy's bed along with the Progress Calendar so they could see quickly what special treat was due.

Had the child been told all about the training? Yes, they had talked about it at the office and on the way home.

Had some special treats been promised for even one or two dry nights? Yes, the milk shake and sundae.

"That's it," said Timmy. "We're all set to go tomorrow. Thanks, Betty, for helping, and you, too, Mom and Dad. I'm going to sleep now so I won't be too tired to practice tomorrow. Good night." He went to bed thinking about all of the special things he would soon be getting.

The next day Timmy returned home early from school so that he could start training. This was the first day of training.

Timmy's mother found the reminder sheet that listed the things to do on this first training day and put it on the table where she could look at it. As soon as Timmy came home, she told him they would get started right away. The first thing to do was to talk about what Timmy would do that day. Betty, his sister, asked if she could watch. Timmy's mother said, "Sure, and you can help, too." Betty was happy to help.

Timmy told his mother he would be drinking a lot and would practice going to the toilet. That he would lie down in bed and pretend he was asleep and practice holding back while lying down. That he would practice rushing to the bathroom when he couldn't hold back anymore. That, before he went to bed, he would learn how to make his bed and to do the getting-up practice. And after he went to bed, he would get up every hour when his mother awakened him to see if he had to go to the bathroom. He forgot to say anything about what he would do if he had an accident, so his mother asked him about that. He knew exactly. He said he would change the sheets and do the getting-up practice.

The first thing to do was for Timmy to start drinking a lot. Timmy's mother had his favorite drinks ready in the refrigerator—milk and Coke. Timmy drank a big glass of milk and then asked if he could go out and play. His mother told him that he should stay inside the house today so that it would be easier to call him every half hour to practice. Betty said she'd help by calling him and offered to go to the store to buy some more milk just in case. Timmy went to the family room to watch TV and play until she got back. Then he would play Monopoly with her. His mother started making dinner. She decided to make something simple today that did not need too much watching so she could interrupt it easily to spend time with Timmy. The time was 3:30.

About fifteen minutes later she went to the family room and offered Timmy some potato chips and peanuts which he ate. That made him thirsty so he had some more milk.

At 4:00 she called Timmy, and he came over right away to the bathroom. She asked Timmy to try to urinate and to tell her when he felt he had to do it. Timmy strained until he felt as if he were going to urinate and told his mother. "OK," she said, "that's good that you have to go. Now rush to your bed and practice holding it back while you are lying down." Timmy still felt that he had to go, but he held his stomach in and held back. His mother followed right behind him as he lay on his bed. She looked at her watch so she could time the two minutes and told Timmy, "You're holding back beautifully. Now, pretend you're asleep and count very, very slowly to fifty, wait a while after each number, and I'll tell you when it's time to get up." Right before Timmy lay down, she asked him, "What will you do if you can't hold it back?" Timmy answered, "I'll get up and rush to the bathroom so I won't wet the bed." "That's right," his mother said.

As Timmy lay on the bed, he closed his eyes and made himself feel very loose and relaxed, and curled up on his side with his legs bent just the way he did when he went to bed at night. Timmy still felt he had to go to the bathroom when he had counted to twenty. But he held back as hard as he could. When he had counted to thirty, though, the feeling was gone. That was about when his mother said, "One more minute to go, you can do it." And he did, because a short while later after he finished counting, his mother told him the time was up and he got up out of bed.

She talked with him about how this holding back would make his bladder stronger, why he should continue drinking, how she would teach him to make his bed, and all the other things he would do. She kept telling him how pleased she was that he held back for so long. She gave him some peanuts and another big glass of milk. He went back to the family room.

Betty had come home and so Timmy started playing Monopoly with her. Mrs. Sander gave him some potato chips about ten minutes later, and again, a few minutes after that. Each time, Timmy also had another drink.

At 4:30, Betty told Timmy it was time to practice again, and she came to the bathroom with Timmy even before their mother reminded them. Again, Timmy was asked to strain until he felt like going. He only strained a little before he felt he was about to go. So quickly, they went to his room where he lay down in bed and again pretended he was asleep. After about one minute he said he couldn't wait. "What should you do then?" his mother asked. Timmy quickly got up and rushed to the bathroom where he urinated. His mother praised him for holding back so long and also for getting up from bed so quickly.

Timmy was proud of himself as he returned to playing with Betty after his mother gave him another drink. She also praised Betty for being so helpful.

Every half hour Timmy was called to the toilet to try to go. Each time, he lay down on his bed and tried some more to hold back. Once he had to go even before he was called by his mother. She had him go to his bed and lie down there again while he tried to hold back. He did hold back and pretty soon didn't have to go anymore.

Timmy's father came home before six o'clock, just in time to see Timmy practicing to hold back in the toilet. He told Timmy he was doing really well.

Dinner was ready soon, and while they ate, they all talked about how well Timmy was holding back and how fast he rushed out of bed to go to the bathroom. Timmy ate hungrily and had another glass and a half of milk during the meal.

Just a few minutes after the meal was over, Timmy's father saw that it was 6:30 and time for the next practice. Timmy went to the bathroom and strained. He had been drinking so much that now it was easy. He felt his tummy feel hard and heavy, and he tried very much to hold back the urine. Again he went to his bed and lay down and tried to wait still longer. When he couldn't wait, he rushed to the bathroom and "went."

Timmy usually went to bed at eight o'clock. At seven o'clock he had another practice in holding back and again he was able to hold it back for the whole two minutes. It was now getting close to bedtime.

Timmy's mother told him that now they would practice what he should do in case he had an accident. First she asked Timmy to tell her once again what he should do. Timmy told her that if he had an accident he would change his pajamas, change the sheets, and do the getting-up practice. Timmy's mother told him how pleased she was that he knew what to do. She gave him more drinks and told him they would then practice cleaning up.

Timmy's mother had him lie down in bed and close his eyes and then she said, "Pretend. Pretend that you had an accident and I just woke you up." She touched him on the shoulder and said, "Timmy, the bed is wet. Show me what you will do." Timmy told her that he would change his clothes. He jumped out of bed. He took off his pajamas and put them in the dirty laundry basket. Then he took his other set of clean pajamas from his dresser and put them on.

Timmy's mother was pleased and told him that was exactly right. "Now I'll show you how to change the bed," she said.

She told Timmy to take off the blanket and sheets and to put the sheets into the dirty laundry basket. Then she told him where the clean sheets were and went with him while he took the clean sheets out of the closet and went back to the bed. She told Timmy that first he would watch her do it, then she would let him make up the bed.

She started putting the sheets on and described out loud to Timmy what she was doing. "First, you spread the sheet on the bed. Then walk around the bed, pulling the sheet so that it hangs down the same on all sides and the bottom. Then, tuck the sheet under the mattress. Walk around the bed, tucking it in and pulling the sheet so it is nice and smooth. Make the corners neat by tucking in one side, then lift the mattress to fold the other side without making the sheet 'bunch up.' " She had him do one side of the bed and two of the corners. Then she put on the top sheet and then the blanket, explaining everything while she did it. And she let him do part of it.

When she was finished, she said, "Now, you do it, Timmy." Timmy did it very slowly since he was not sure, but his mother told him he was doing it just fine and reminded him what to do next. She was so proud. He was doing it slowly, and so she started to do it for him, but he said, "Let me do it myself, please, Mommy," and she readily agreed. When he had some trouble with the corners and with making the sheet smooth, instead of doing it for him, she told him how to do it and guided his hand for a moment.

Finally, Timmy was finished. Timmy's mother called his sister and father in to see what he had done. They all told him how smooth and neat the bed looked and what a good job he had done. Timmy was very pleased with himself.

"Now," his mother said, "let's do the getting-up practice. Remember how you are supposed to do it? You lie down in bed and pretend you are asleep. Then you will try to make yourself feel like you have to go even just a little bit. You'll jump up very, very quickly. If you can't make yourself feel like you have to go, then think real hard and try to remember what it feels like. As soon as you can remember, then quickly jump up. Go to the bathroom fast and try to go to the toilet. Then come back to bed and start all over again. How many times do you do this, Timmy?" Timmy told her, "Twenty times." "That's right," Timmy's mother said as he lay down on the bed for the first practice.

"Now, Timmy, I want you to count out loud so I can hear you—softly, but just loud enough for me to hear," Timmy's mother told him. "Close your eyes; that's right. And you can be on your side with your legs pulled up a little, the way you usually do. And breathe real deep and slow just the way you see me do when I'm asleep." Timmy did as he was told and began counting, "One, two, three, four," and so on. "A little more slowly and that will be perfect," his mother said softly. Timmy continued more slowly, "Eleven . . . twelve . . . thirteen . . ." and so on much more slowly until he reached the number fifty. Then he stopped.

Timmy tried to make himself feel as if he had to go to the bathroom. In a few seconds he started feeling like it and immediately jumped up and ran to the bathroom where he really did go. When he came back, his mother told him he did it perfectly and to start the second practice.

On the next few practices he counted quietly to himself, and pretty soon he didn't have to count at all because he could tell how long he had to wait. Also, on the next few practices, he couldn't make himself feel as if he had to urinate. So he thought about some other times when he really felt like going, and jumped up as soon as he thought of how it felt.

Timmy's mother stood near the door of the bedroom all the time and told Timmy how well he was doing on each practice. Timmy counted the number of practices. Each time he came back to his bed from the bathroom he would call out, "One," or "Two," or "Three." Finally, on the last practice, he called out "Twenty," and said, "Boy, I'm tired." Betty and his father also told Timmy how well he had done.

By now it was close to Timmy's bedtime. As he climbed into bed, his mother sat on the edge of the bed to talk to him and to give him the bedtime reminders.

First, she asked him to repeat what he should do if he had an accident tonight. Timmy told her that he would change his clothes, change the bed, and do the getting-up practice.

Then she reminded him that she would be waking him up every hour for him to go to the toilet if he had to. Timmy told her he would wake up right away as soon as she asked him to.

Timmy then drank some more, about half a glass of milk. Then Timmy felt the sheets, running his hands over them and thinking about how dry they felt. His mother talked with him about the milk shake and sundae and other nice things he would be receiving if he was dry. She reminded him to think about how his tummy felt and asked him what he would do if he felt as if he had to urinate. "I'll get up real fast," he said, "and I'll run to the bathroom." His mother gave him a kiss, said good night, and left the room. As she left, she started to close the door but left it open when she realized that Timmy would have an easier time getting to the bathroom if it was not closed as it usually was.

An hour later, Timmy's mother came into the bedroom and saw him sound asleep. She felt the blanket and was delighted to find that the bed was dry. She softly said, "Timmy, Timmy," but he didn't answer. She touched his shoulder, but still Timmy didn't move. So she started to raise him, but he opened his eyes and sat up. She talked to him until he looked her in the eye and seemed awake and attentive. "What are you supposed to do now, Timmy?" she asked. "Can you hold it another hour or do you want to go to the bathroom?" Timmy felt as if he'd better go, and said so as he quickly got out of bed and went to the bathroom. His mother told him that he did the right thing if he felt as if he had to.

When Timmy returned, he drank some more, then got into bed where he again felt the sheets and thought how dry they were. Again, his mother told him to think about his tummy and asked him what he would do if he felt he had to go. He told her, and then fell asleep as he thought about how he should get up.

At the next awakening an hour later, Timmy woke up as soon as his mother touched his shoulder and the time after that he sat up as soon as he heard his name called.

The first two times he was awakened he got up and went to the bathroom. The next time he didn't feel as if he had to go so he said he would wait even after his mother asked if he was sure. She told him she was glad he was able to hold back so long.

At the eleven o'clock awakening, Timmy's mother did not give him any more drinks. He was so sleepy anyhow that he didn't feel too thirsty now. She thought that the last awakening would be at one o'clock, but then Timmy's father said that he would stay up until two o'clock and give Timmy another wake-up just to make sure.

Timmy's bed was dry at each of the awakenings. He had gotten up to go to the bathroom on all but two of them. After the last awakening at two o'clock, his dad went to sleep, too. His sister had gone to sleep much earlier and his mother just an hour ago. The first day of training was over.

Timmy's mother was very nervous when she went to check his bed the next morning to see if it was dry. She thought to herself that with all those drinks it would be a miracle. She checked while Timmy was still asleep at 7:00 A.M., a half hour before his usual wake-up time at 7:30.

Timmy's bed was dry! She quickly woke up Betty and Timmy's father and told them the good news. She made an extra-special breakfast of pancakes and sausages, which was Timmy's favorite.

This was the first dry night that Timmy had ever had and that called for a celebration.

They all went into Timmy's bedroom at 7:30 to wake him up and tell him the good news. When he was awake, they all clapped their hands and hugged him. Then they clapped again as Timmy wrote "Dry" in big letters on his Calendar Progress chart. That meant a big milk shake today.

At breakfast, they all talked about how Timmy had finally learned to stay dry and all because he had tried so hard and practiced so hard. Timmy's father said he would like to take Betty along to the ice cream store, too, and get her something for being such a big help.

It was Saturday and no school. After breakfast Timmy had to go to the bathroom and almost forgot that now he was supposed to hold back as long as he could. He was able to wait about twenty minutes. Then he did it in the measuring cup when he couldn't wait much longer. Timmy's mother showed him how to read the number on the cup and they wrote it down. He had held back a long time and his mother and father told Timmy he was starting off very nicely.

Timmy played outside during most of the day. Each time that he felt that he had to go to the bathroom he told himself to wait. He found that if he could make himself wait for even a little while, then he didn't have to go. Each time he did go to the bathroom, he did it in the measuring cup and showed it to his mother. She was pleased at how much he did and wrote it down on the paper in the bathroom. Then she emptied the cup.

When Timmy did a very big amount in the cup, his mother always gave him something special like a cookie or ice cream. In fact, even when he didn't do an extra amount in the cup, she was pleased that he was trying so hard and always told him.

At dinner they all again told Timmy how proud they were of him. Then they went to the ice cream store where Timmy got his big milk shake. Dad gave Betty a milk shake, too.

At bedtime that night, Timmy looked at the Happy Clock. He drew the hand in to point at twelve o'clock. That was when his mother would wake him up tonight to go to the toilet. That was the time when she usually went to sleep. She and Dad were going out to a party tonight and would be back about eleven o'clock.

After Timmy "set" the Happy Clock, his mother reminded him about getting up if he had to go at night and also what he should do if he found the bed wet. He felt the sheets and thought hard about his tummy. He decided he felt a little bit like going to the bathroom so he got up right then and went even before his mother asked him to.

At twelve o'clock, when his mother and father checked his bed, it was dry. They awakened Timmy then and had him go to the bathroom.

Timmy was dry the next morning, too. That was two nights in a row. They all looked at the written agreement and saw that meant a sundae for him today. Timmy wrote down "Dry" again on his Calendar Progress Chart in the morning, and also penciled in the Happy Clock to show 11:30.

He was dry again the next night. That was three dry nights in a row. That meant a call to Grandma. Timmy's mother called her and said she had some wonderful news to tell her about Timmy's bedwetting. She would let Timmy tell her himself. Timmy was bubbling with excitement as he told her. Grandma kept telling him how excited she was, too, and said she would come over and visit soon to see him.

Timmy was dry the next night, too. All this time he was using the measuring cup and trying very hard to hold back as long as he could so that he could get as much in the cup as he could. And every day, especially at each meal, his mother and dad told him he was doing great. Betty helped, too, by reading from the cup when his mother wasn't there when he went to the bathroom. Each night before he went to bed he penciled in a bigger part of the Happy Clock. So, after the fourth dry night he now would be awakened at nine o'clock, just one hour and a half after he went to bed.

On the fifth night, when Timmy was awakened, the bed was wet. Timmy was so upset he almost started to cry. But his mother told him not to cry. She was sad that the bed was wet, but now he knew what to do to correct it. As his mother watched, he changed his clothes and then remade the bed, putting the clean sheets on. Then he did the getting-up practice. It was about ten o'clock and he was sleepy, but he knew that this practice would help him to stay dry the rest of the night. When he finished, his mother told him that she was sure his practice would help him to stay dry and she gave him the same reminders as before. That night, when everyone was asleep, he got up all by himself when he started dreaming about going to the toilet. In the morning, his bed was dry.

Before breakfast, he sadly wrote "Wet" on his calendar, but his mother and dad and Betty all told him that just one "Wet" after four dry nights was wonderful and they were sure he would be dry again. That night he missed part of his playtime because he had to start his getting-up practice a half hour before bedtime. Timmy didn't like stopping the playing with his friend, but he knew that by practicing he would be able to keep dry that night. At bedtime he didn't color in the Happy Clock since the clock should be colored only if the bed was dry the night before. Timmy did his getting-up practice and tried real hard. Each time he lay on his bed he thought to himself, Tonight if I have to go even a little bit I'm going to hold it back no matter what! And I'll get up so fast!

And he was right. That night he was dry. He was dry when his mother woke him up to go to the bathroom. And he was still dry in the morning. "We knew the other night was just an accident and that you could do it, Timmy," his mother said. And Betty and Dad agreed. He wrote "Dry" in big letters on his calendar that morning. And that night, before bedtime, he was smiling when he colored in the Happy Clock earlier by another half hour.

That was five nights he had been dry. His agreement was that when he was dry for five nights, he could throw away the plastic sheet on his mattress. When he took it off, he asked his mother if he should save it just in case. She said, "No, Timmy, let's throw it away. You might have one or two more wettings by accident, but I don't think we really need it." Timmy put the sheet in the trash can.

The next night he was dry again. That was six nights and the agreement said that now he could have a new pair of pajamas. That afternoon he went with his mother to the store and Timmy picked out a pair of pajamas with big stripes just like the ones he saw his friends wear.

And the next night he was dry again. Seven nights. That meant he could call Larry to come sleep over next Friday or Saturday. He called and Larry was glad to come. He had never stayed over with Timmy before. No one had.

Three more nights Timmy was dry and that meant he got a sleeping bag. Dad had said no more than $20. But when Dad saw one sleeping bag on sale for $30 that had down feathers in it, he told Timmy to get it anyhow. He had been dry for six nights in a row now!

But, then, another accident. That happened soon after the awakening at night had stopped. And now he had to hold back all night long. So, the next morning he changed the bed and did the getting-up practice. And the next night he did the practice again a half hour before bedtime. It worked and he was dry again.

Timmy's mother knew that the getting-up practice was

a lot of work for Timmy. So, she was surprised when Timmy told her the next night that he wanted to do the practice before he went to bed even though he didn't have to. He wanted to be sure that he would be dry that night.

During the daytime he tried very hard to hold back and to go to the bathroom as few times as he could. So, each time he used the measuring cup he was able to see that he could hold more and more.

Two weeks went by without any wettings since Timmy had that last accident. When twelve days had passed, the agreement said that he could go to Auntie Susan's to visit overnight. Mom called and she set a date. Mom told her not to worry about Timmy wetting the bed because now he was dry every night.

Two weeks of dryness was when Timmy didn't have to use the measuring cup anymore. But he decided that he would still hold back as long as he could so he would be able to hold back easier at night, too.

The next night he was dry again. That was fifteen nights and that was extraspecial. Timmy's father called the camp director and told him that Timmy was going to go to camp that summer. His father wrote out a check and a letter for the summer camp and Timmy put it in the mailbox. "I'm going to have so much fun!" he shouted.

Timmy had one more accident three days later and then another one three weeks after that. He was very sad each time he had one. But he knew what to do each time. He changed the sheets and did the twenty getting-up practices. And his mother did not get angry or look so sad anymore.

Betty stopped teasing him. And Dad was so proud of him. His mother and father told him one day as they looked at the Progress Calendar, "Timmy, we want to buy you a new bed, a bigger one. You are getting to be a young man now and we're not worried about the bed being ruined anymore. So this weekend we'll go to the furniture store and we'll choose a new bed together." Timmy wondered if that new bed was in the agreements. "No," his mother said, "that's an extra thing we want you to have."

Timmy kept on writing on the Progress Calendar each morning. But, after one whole month went by, he stopped. He soon forgot that he ever had wet his bed.

One day, one of the friends who had teased him before said, "Say, Timmy, do you still wet your bed?"

"Of course not," Timmy answered quickly. "That was a long, long, long time ago!"

m.n
pot. chips
ice cream
soda
juice

Appendix 1

REMINDER LIST OF PREPARATIONS FOR TRAINING

	(Circle Answer)	
1. Is the child old enough?	Yes	No
2. Has the child stopped pants-wetting during the day?	Yes	No
3. If the problem seems medical, has a physician been consulted?	Yes	No
4. Do you have ample amounts of the child's favorite drinks and snack treats?	Yes	No
5. Is there a night-light in the hall and enough light in the bedroom for the child to be able to find the way to the toilet?	Yes	No
6. Has the child's bed been placed in a location convenient for him to get to the toilet and for making his bed?	Yes	No

7. Have the other children at home been informed of the training effort and told how to help?	Yes	No
8. If you have decided to use a pad-and-buzzer apparatus, have you obtained one and learned how to use it?	Yes	No
9. Have you obtained a measuring cup for your child?	Yes	No
10. Do you have a Calendar Progress Chart?	Yes	No
11. Have you chosen a convenient day for training?	Yes	No
12. Have both parents agreed on the training plan?	Yes	No
13. Are the child's nightclothes easy to remove for toileting?	Yes	No
14. Has a written agreement been made with the child regarding the benefits the child will receive?	Yes	No
15. Has the child been told about all of the training procedures and the reasons for each of them?	Yes	No
16. In the written agreement, have benefits been arranged for even one or two dry nights as well as for longer-term dryness?	Yes	No

Appendix 2

OUTLINE OF
THE TRAINING PROCEDURES
ON THE INTENSIVE
TRAINING DAY

I. DURING THE AFTERNOON
   A. Parent reviews the procedures with the child and asks child to repeat them to show his understanding.
   B. The child is encouraged to drink large amounts of his favorite drinks.
   C. Every half hour the child is requested to attempt urination.
      1. If the child feels the need to urinate, he is encouraged to hold it back as long as he can until the urge goes away.
      2. If the urge to urinate remains, the child lies on his bed as if asleep, then arises and goes to the bathroom, to urinate in the cup, acting out what he should do at night.
      3. The child is praised for his efforts, whether or not he urinated, and is given more drinks.

II. ONE HOUR BEFORE BEDTIME

A. Parent reviews with the child the procedures of correcting accidents.

B. Parent continues to encourage the child to drink.

C. Child acts out the procedures to be followed after an accident.
1. Child is required to change his own nightclothes.
2. Child removes sheets and puts them back on himself.

D. Child acts out the getting-up practice.
1. Child lies down in bed as if asleep.
2. Child counts to self.
3. Child arises and hurries to the bathroom.
4. Child attempts to urinate in the measuring cup.
5. Child returns to bed.
6. Child repeats above steps—1, 2, 3, 4, and 5—twenty times while parent counts the trials.

III. AT BEDTIME

A. Bedtime scheduled earlier than usual.

B. The parent reviews the procedure to be followed on accident correction and scheduled awakenings and the child restates these requirements.

C. Child continues to drink.

D. The parents review with the child the benefits promised for dryness and express their confidence in the child.

E. The child feels the sheets and comments on their dryness.

F. The child retires for the night.

IV. AFTER THE CHILD IS IN BED

A. Awaken the child every hour until midnight or 1:00 A.M.

B. Use a minimal prompt to awaken the child.

C. Determine whether the bed is wet.

D. If the bed is dry:

    1. Ask the child whether he can wait or whether he must urinate.

        a) If the child is able to wait another hour:

            (1) Praise his urinary control.

        b) If the child feels he must urinate:

            (1) Child goes to bathroom to urinate in the cup.

            (2) Praise child for his preventive action.

            (3) Child returns to bed.

        c) Child feels the bed sheets and comments on dryness.

        d) Praise child for having a dry bed.

        e) Give child more drinks (discontinue after 10:00 or 11:00 P.M.).

        f) Child returns to sleep.

E. If the bed is wet:

    1. Awaken the child and mildly reprimand for wetting.

    2. Child feels wet sheets and comments on wetness.

    3. Child goes to bathroom to finish urinating.

    4. Child changes into dry nightclothes.

    5. Child removes wet sheets and places in dirty laundry.

    6. Child obtains dry sheets and remakes the bed.

    7. Child performs getting-up practice for twenty trials.

    8. Remind child to awaken half hour earlier in morning and to do getting-up practice before bedtime tomorrow.

    9. Child feels bed sheets and comments on dryness.

    10. Praise child for correcting the wetness.

    11. Child returns to sleep.

V. INSPECT THE BED FOR DRYNESS ONE HALF HOUR EARLIER THE NEXT MORNING.

Appendix 3

OUTLINE OF
THE CONTINUING PRACTICE
AFTER THE INTENSIVE
TRAINING DAY

I. HOLDING-BACK PRACTICE
   A. Child uses measuring cup for every urination.
   B. Write down the amount of urination.
   C. Praise the child for his short-term and long-term progress at each urination.
      1. If younger child, give small snack treat as reward.

II. NIGHTLY AWAKENING
   A. Awaken child once during night.
      1. Use minimal prompt when awakening.
      2. Inspect bed for wetness.
      3. Child feels sheets and comments on dryness or wetness.
      4. Child goes to the bathroom, urinates in the cup, and returns to bed.
      5. Child feels sheets again.

    6. Child states what he will do if he feels urge to urinate.

    7. Express confidence to child as child returns to sleep.

B. Adjust time of the nightly awakening (see Happy Clock).

    1. On first night, awaken child at parents' bedtime.

    2. If child is dry, awaken him one half hour earlier the next night.

    3. If child is wet, awaken him at the same time the next night.

C. If child is wet at the nightly awakening:

    1. Gently reprimand child and have child feel wet sheets.

      a) Child changes nightclothes, changes sheets.

      b) Child performs getting-up practice for twenty trials.

      c) Child returns to sleep after feeling dry sheets and describing what he will do if he has the urge to urinate.

      d) Praise child for practice and express confidence in future success.

      e) Remind the child to perform the getting-up practice again before his bedtime the next day.

III. CALENDAR PROGRESS CHART

A. Each morning have child record previous night's wetness or dryness.

    1. Discuss with child the progress made.

    2. Both parents discuss progress with child.

    3. Relate the progress to the benefits and rewards listed in the agreements.

IV. AT BEDTIME

A. Child feels sheets and comments on their dryness.

B. Child describes what he will do if he has urge to urinate.

C. Child describes his current need to urinate.
D. Express confidence in child and review his progress.
E. Discuss how the child's progress is related to the rewards listed in the agreements.

V. MORNING BED INSPECTION—one half hour earlier than usual awakening
   A. If bed is dry, do not awaken child.
   B. If bed is wet, child performs usual changing and getting-up practice.
   C. Calendar Progress Chart and Happy Clock are marked as to wet or dry.

VI. ONE HALF HOUR BEFORE USUAL BEDTIME
   A. If child was wet previous night, child performs getting-up practice.

VII. DURING DAY
   A. Child and parents describe progress to relevant friend or family members.
   B. Parents repeatedly express confidence in child and praise him.
   C. Review written agreement of benefits and provide them as promised.

Appendix 4

OUTLINE FOR
PHASING OUT
THE TRAINING PROGRAM

I. NIGHTLY AWAKENINGS
  A. Nightly awakening occurs one half hour earlier after each dry night.
    1. When nightly awakening is within one hour of bedtime, discontinue the nightly awakenings entirely.
    2. Eliminate Happy Clock when nightly awakenings are discontinued.

II. HOLDING-BACK PRACTICE
  A. After *fourteen straight nights of dryness*, discontinue need for child to urinate in measuring cup.
  B. Encourage child on his own to hold back urine as long as possible.

III. CALENDAR PROGRESS CHART
   A. Discontinue recording on Calendar Progress Chart after *one straight month of dryness.*

IV. MORNING INSPECTIONS OF BED
   A. Discontinue early-morning inspections after *one straight month of dryness.*

V. BEDTIME AWARENESS PROCEDURE
   A. Discontinue feeling of sheets and thought rehearsal after *one straight month of dryness.*

VI. PRAISE FOR BEING DRY
   A. Gradually decrease after the first two weeks of dryness.

VII. PAD-AND-BUZZER APPARATUS (IF USED)
   A. Discontinue apparatus after two weeks of dryness.

VIII. PROCEDURES WHICH WILL NOT BE PHASED OUT
   A. Child changes clothes and remakes bed after an accident.
   B. Child does getting-up practice before bedtime if there was an accident the night before, as well as doing the practice when the accident was discovered.

Appendix 5

SUPPLIERS OF THE PAD-AND-BUZZER APPARATUS

1. Sears, Roebuck, Catalog No. 8G1164 (Wee-Alert Buzzer). Approximate cost, $28.
2. Montgomery Ward, Catalog No. 53B21530 (Wet-Guard Kit). Approximate cost, $28.

Appendix 6

DRY-BED
HAPPY CLOCK

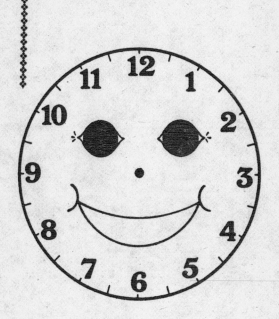

Appendix 7

DRY-BED CALENDAR

MON	TUES	WED	THURS	FRI	SAT	SUN

Appendix 7 (*continued*)

DRY-BED CALENDAR

MON	TUES	WED	THURS	FRI	SAT	SUN

Appendix 8

SELF-TEST QUESTIONS

Circle the correct answer for each question. The correct answers can be found on page 177.

1. How old should the child be before training?
   a) 2 yrs. b) 3 yrs. c) 6 yrs.

2. Should training be started if the child has many accidents during the day?
   a) Yes b) No

3. Should a physician be consulted before training if there seems to be a medical problem?
   a) Yes b) No

4. If the child has a slight cold, should training be started?
   a) Yes b) No

5. Should training be started if the husband and wife do not agree with the need for this method of training?
   a) Yes b) No

6. The family is going on a vacation in 2 weeks. Can training start now anyhow?
   a) Yes b) No

7. Should the child continue to wear diapers at night during training?
   a) Yes b) No

8. If the child is still using a potty chair, and not the regular toilet, can training still be started?
   a) Yes b) No

9. Should the other children in the family be told about the training?
   a) Yes b) No

10. What should the other children in the family be asked to do about the training? Should they
    a) Stay out of it? b) Help? c) Watch, but not talk about it?

11. If the toilet is on a different floor, and the child can't walk the stairs, should training start anyhow?
    a) Yes b) No

12. How far should the child's bed be from the walls?
    a) Doesn't matter b) A foot or more c) Touching wall

13. The hallway from the bedroom to the toilet should
    a) Be dark b) Have some light

14. If 2 children are bedwetting, should training be started for both at the same time?
    a) Yes b) No

15. If 2 children are bedwetting, which child should be trained first?
    a) The older b) the younger

16. If another child sleeps in the same room, can training be started anyhow?
    a) Yes b) No

17. If the child is about 15 or 16 years old, should this training procedure be used?
    a) Yes b) No

18. If the child is 6 years old, about what are the chances that he will outgrow the bedwetting problem during the next year?
    a) 9 chances out of 10   b) 5 out of 10   c) 2 out of 10

19. How much should the child be told about the details and reasons for the training?
    a) Very little b) What to do, but not why c) What to do and why

20. When should the child be told about the training?
    a) Once training starts b) Beforehand

21. Will the trainer have to get up in the middle of the night to do this training?
    a) Yes b) No

22. Should all of the training procedures be started
    a) On the same day? b) Can they be added one day at a time?

23. Should
    a) All of the recommended procedures be used? b) Can some be omitted?

24. Is the pad and buzzer
    a) Required? b) Recommended? c) Not useful?

25. Should the parent schedule any other activities during the first training day?
    a) Yes b) No

26. What supplies are needed before starting training?
    a) Drinks, snacks, measuring cup b) Measuring cup
    c) None

27. When giving drinks on the first day should one use
    a) Different types of drinks? b) One type?

28. On the first training day should the snack treats be
    a) Salty? b) Sweet?

29. On the first afternoon that training starts, should the child play
    a) Outdoors? b) Indoors?

30. On the first night of training should the child have extra drinks up until
    a) Suppertime? b) His bedtime? c) 2 hours before the parents' bedtime?

31. On the first training night, how often should the child be awakened?
    a) Every hour b) Every half hour c) Every 2 hours

32. Is awareness development during sleep one of the basic objectives of treatment?
    a) Yes b) No

33. Is increasing bladder control a basic objective of treatment?
    a) Yes b) No

34. Is practice in nighttime toileting optional?
    a) Yes b) No

35. Recording on a Calendar Progress Chart is
    a) Optional b) Required

36. On the first day of training, should a contract of benefits for staying dry at night be made just for
    a) Long-term success? b) Even 1 or 2 days' success?
    c) Both long- and short-term success?

37. On the first day of training, should the list of inconveniences of being wet at night be
    a) Discussed with your child? b) Ignored?

38. On the first day of training, should
    a) The child make his own bed? b) The parent?

39. On the first day of training should the urine be measured
    a) Once? b) Each time the child urinates?

40. On the first training day, when the child has the urge to go, should one encourage the child
    a) To toilet immediately? b) To hold back?

41. On the first training day, should the child return to play if the urge to urinate is gone?
    a) Yes b) No

42. On the first training day should the holding-back procedure be practiced
    a) Until suppertime? b) Until bedtime?

43. On the first training day after lying down, if the urge persists after 2 minutes should the child jump up and go?
    a) Yes b) No

44. Should the child look at a clock to time his holding-back duration?
    a) Yes b) No

45. When should measuring of urine be done?
    a) Only on the first day of training b) Until the child is dry for 2 weeks

46. On the first day of training should the parent be
    a) Next to the child? b) In a different room?

47. On the first night of training should the child be awakened
    a) Only at midnight? b) Each hour until midnight?

48. If the child is very slow to awaken, should the parent
    a) Persist? b) Let him sleep?

49. If on the hourly inspection on the first night of training, the child is wet, shall the parent
    a) Let him sleep? b) Change his sheets? c) Let him change his sheets?

50. On the hourly inspection on the first night of training, if the child is wet should he do the getting-up practice
    a) As soon as he changes the sheets? b) Wait until the next day?

51. If the pad and buzzer is used and it signals an accident, should the parent
    a) Let the buzzer awaken the child? b) Help the child awaken?

52. When should the bedtime story about bedwetting be read?
    a) Before the first night of training b) After the first night

53. Should the child be spanked for having an accident?
    a) Yes b) No

54. On the first night should bedtime be set
    a) Earlier by one half hour? b) At usual bedtime? c) One half hour later?

55. Should the child stroke the sheets and comment on their dryness before going to bed
    a) Each night? b) Only on training night?

56. Should the getting-up practice be used
    a) Only on the first training night? b) Whenever a bed-wetting accident is discovered?

57. If there has been an accident, should the getting-up procedure be used
    a) Again before bedtime the next night? b) Only after the accident?

58. Should the snacks and drinking of liquids be given
    a) On the second night after training? b) Only on the first night of training? c) The rest of the week?

59. Should the child be praised when the measured amount of urine
    a) Sets a record? b) Is very large? c) For every attempt?

60. During the day should the child's drinking be
    a) Restricted? b) Not restricted?

61. If the child becomes upset and refuses to do the getting-up practice, should the child
    a) Be allowed to skip it? b) Think about it and then do it? c) Be forced to do it immediately?

62. If the child is upset and refuses to do the getting-up practice after an accident, even after thinking about it for several minutes, should he be allowed to
    a) Skip it? b) Think about it some more and then do it? c) Be spanked and forced to do it?

63. While the child is "thinking about it" after having an accident, should he be
    a) Watching TV? b) Playing? c) Sitting and thinking alone?

64. Should the bed be inspected each morning a half hour before waking-up time?
    a) Yes b) No

65. Should the nightly awakening be discontinued when
    a) The Happy Clock is pointed at the child's bedtime? b) 1 hour after the child's bedtime? c) At the parents' bedtime?

66. Should the Happy Clock nightly awakening time be moved
    a) Toward bedtime? b) Away from it?

67. Should the child's wetness or dryness each day be recorded on the Progress Chart
    a) By the child? b) By the parent?

68. Should the parent discuss the Progress Chart with the child
    a) When there has been an accident? b) Every night?

69. After the first training night, is the nightly awakening done
    a) Once a night? b) Several times each night?

70. After the training day, should the child continue to use the measuring cup for
    a) Every urination? b) Just before bedtime? c) Only when the parent is at home?

71. Who should write down the amount of measured urine in the cup?
    a) The parent b) The child

72. Should snack treats be given as a reward for
    a) Each large amount of measured urine? b) Only when a record is set?

73. After the first training day, when the child is awakened at the nightly awakening, should he
    a) Stroke sheets? b) Go urinate in bathroom? c) Describe his future actions if he has the urge later? d) All of the above—stroke sheets, go urinate, describe intentions?

74. If the child is wet, is the time of nightly awakening the next night
    a) Moved one half hour later? b) Kept at the same time? c) Moved one half hour earlier?

75. If the child is dry, is the time of awakening the next night
    a) Moved one half hour later? b) Kept at same time? c) Moved one half hour earlier?

76. When the child is found to have an accident, how many getting-up practice trials does he do?
     a) 1 b) 5 c) 20

77. When the child is doing the getting-up practice and changing the sheets after an accident, the parent should stay next to the child
     a) Only on the first few days b) After every accident

78. After an accident, the child
     a) Strokes the sheets? b) Changes the sheets? c) Strokes and changes the sheets?

79. After an accident, the parent shows
     a) Disapproval of wetness? b) Confidence in future efforts with no disapproval? c) Disapproval of wetness and confidence in future efforts?

80. If the bed is found dry at the morning inspection, the child is
     a) Awakened and praised b) Allowed to sleep c) Awakened, praised, and returned to sleep

81. After an accident, the child practices the getting-up exercise the next night
     a) At his usual bedtime b) A half hour before the usual bedtime

82. The morning inspections are made by the parent until the child has
     a) 1 dry night b) 1 week of dryness c) 1 month of dryness

83. After one straight month of dryness, discontinue
     a) The morning inspections b) The bedtime feeling of sheets and thought rehearsal c) Progress Calendar recording d) all of the above

84. The measuring cup records of urination should be discontinued after
    a) 1 night of dryness b) 2 weeks of dryness c) 3 months of dryness

85. The changing of sheets by the child after an accident should be discontinued
    a) After 1 week of dryness b) 1 month of dryness c) Never discontinued

86. The getting-up practice after an accident should be discontinued
    a) After 1 month of dryness b) After 3 months of dryness c) Never discontinued

87. The list of agreed-upon benefits for dryness should be posted
    a) In the bathroom b) Next to the Progress Chart c) In the kitchen

88. The Calendar Progress Chart is posted in the
    a) Bedroom b) Kitchen c) Bathroom

89. The rewards and benefits listed in the agreement should be
    a) Saved up and given when it is convenient b) given one at a time as soon as each one is earned

90. If an accident occurs after 2 months of dryness, should one
    a) Omit the practice unless wetting persists? b) Reintroduce the cleaning up and practice right away?

SELF-TEST ANSWERS

1) b.	24) b.	47) b.	69) a.
2) b.	25) b.	48) a.	70) a.
3) a.	26) a.	49) c.	71) b.
4) b.	27) a.	50) a.	72) a.
5) b.	28) a.	51) b.	73) d.
6) b.	29) b.	52) a.	74) b.
7) b.	30) c.	53) b.	75) c.
8) a.	31) a.	54) a.	76) c.
9) a.	32) a.	55) a.	77) a.
10) b.	33) a.	56) b.	78) c.
11) b.	34) b.	57) a.	79) c.
12) b.	35) b.	58) b.	80) b.
13) b.	36) c.	59) c.	81) b.
14) b.	37) a.	60) b.	82) c.
15) a.	38) a.	61) b.	83) d.
16) a.	39) b.	62) b.	84) b.
17) a.	40) b.	63) c.	85) c.
18) c.	41) a.	64) a.	86) c.
19) c.	42) b.	65) b.	87) b.
20) b.	43) a.	66) a.	88) a.
21) b.	44) b.	67) a.	89) b.
22) a.	45) b.	68) b.	90) b.
23) a.	46) a.		

References

I. REVIEW OF STUDIES OF THE OCCURRENCE OF BEDWETTING
Lovibond, S. H. *Conditioning and Enuresis*. Elmsford, N.Y.: Pergamon Press, 1964.

II. BEDWETTING IN INSTITUTIONALIZED POPULATIONS
Baller, W. R., and Giangreco, J. C. "Correction of Nocturnal Enuresis in Deaf Children," *The Volta Review*, 7 (1970):545–47.

Jehu, D.; Morgan, R. T. T.; Turner, R. K.; and Jones, A. "A Controlled Trial of the Treatment of Nocturnal Enuresis in Residential Homes for Children." *Behavior Research and Therapy* 15 (1977):1–16.

Kaffman, M. "Enuresis Among Kibbutz Children." *Harefuah* 62 (1962):251–53.

———. Toilet-Training by Multiple Caretakers: Enuresis Among Kibbutz Children." *Israel Annals of Psychiatry and Related Disciplines* 10 (1972):341–65.

Mowrer, O., and Mowrer, W. M. "Enuresis: A Method for Its Study and Treatment." *American Journal of Orthopsychiatry* 8 (1938):436–47.

Thorne, F. C. "The Incidence of Nocturnal Enuresis After Age Five." *American Journal of Psychiatry* 100 (1944):686–89.

III. HISTORY OF TREATMENTS FOR BEDWETTING

Glicklich, L. B. "An Historical Account of Enuresis." *Pediatrics* 8 (1951):859–75.

IV. INVENTION OF THE PAD-AND-BUZZER METHOD

Mowrer, O., and Mowrer, W. M. "Enuresis: A Method for Its Study and Treatment." *American Journal of Orthopsychiatry* 8 (1938):436–47.

V. COMPARISON OF DRUG TREATMENT AND PAD-AND-BUZZER TREATMENT OF BEDWETTING

McConaghy, N. "A Controlled Trial of Imipramine, Amphetamine, Pad-and-Bell Conditioning and Random Awakening in the Treatment of Nocturnal Enuresis." *The Medical Journal of Australia* (1969):237–39.

Shaffer, D.; Costello, A. J.; and Hill, I. D. "Control of Enuresis with Imipramine." *Archives of Disease in Childhood* 43 (1968):665–71.

VI. REVIEWS OF STUDIES OF THE PAD-AND-BUZZER TREATMENT OF BEDWETTING

Collins, R. W. "Importance of Bladder-Cue Buzzer Contingency in the Conditioning Treatment for Enuresis." *Journal of Abnormal Psychology* 82 (1973): 299–308.

Jones, H. G. "The Behavioural Treatment of Enuresis Nocturna." In *Behaviour Therapy and the Neuroses*, edited by H. J. Eysenck, Elmsford, N.Y.: Pergamon Press, 1960, pp. 337–403.

Lovibond, S. H. *Conditioning and Enuresis*. Elmsford, N.Y.: Pergamon Press, 1964.

Yates, A. J. *Behavior Therapy*. New York: John Wiley, 1970.

VII. COMPARISONS OF PSYCHOTHERAPY WITH THE PAD-AND-BUZZER TREATMENT OF BEDWETTING

DeLeon, G., and Mandell, W. "A Comparison of Conditioning and Psychotherapy in the Treatment of Functional Enuresis." *Journal of Clinical Psychology* 22 (1966):326–30.

Werry, J., and Cohrssen, J. "Enuresis—An Etiologic and Therapeutic Study." *The Journal of Pediatrics* 67 (1965):423–31.

VIII. NONTECHNICAL DISCUSSION OF MEDICAL ASPECTS OF BEDWETTING

Rowan, R. L. *Bed-Wetting, A Guide for Parents*. New York: St. Martin's Press, 1974.

IX. BLADDER CAPACITY INCREASED BY TRAINING

Hagglund, T. B. "Enuretic Children Treated with Fluid Restriction or Forced Drinking." *Annals Paediatriae Fenniae* 11 (1965):84.

Muellner, S. R. "Development of Urinary Control in Children." *Journal of the American Medical Association* 172 (1960):1256.

Paschalis, A. P.; Kimmel, H. D.; and Kimmel, E. "Further Study of Diurnal Instrumental Conditioning in the Treatment of Enuresis Nocturna." *Journal of Behavior Therapy and Experimental Psychiatry* 3 (1972):253–56.

Starfield, B., and Mellits, E. D. "Increase in Functional Bladder Capacity and Improvements in Enuresis." *The Journal of Pediatrics* 72 (1968):483–87.

X. RETARDED PERSONS TREATED FOR BEDWETTING BY THE PRESENT METHOD

Azrin, N. H., and Foxx, R. M. "A Rapid Method of Toilet Training the Institutionalized Retarded." *Journal of Applied Behavior Analysis* 4 (1971):89–99.

Foxx, R. M., and Azrin, N. H. *Toilet Training the Retarded: A Rapid Program for Day and Nighttime Independent Toileting.* Champaign, Ill.: Research Press, 1973.

XI. DAYTIME TOILET TRAINING

Azrin, N. H., and Foxx, R. M. *Toilet Training in Less Than a Day.* New York: Simon and Schuster, 1974.

Foxx, R. M., and Azrin, N. H. "Dry Pants: A Rapid Method of Toilet Training Children." *Behavior Research and Therapy* 11 (1973):435–42.

Butler, J. F. "The Toilet Training Success of Parents After Reading 'Toilet Training in Less Than a Day.' " *Behavior Therapy* 7 (1976):185–91.

XII. THE PRESENT METHOD OF TREATING BEDWETTING

Azrin, N. H.; Hontos, P. T.; and Besalel-Azrin, V. B. "Elimination of Enuresis Without a Conditioning Apparatus: An Extension by Office Instruction of the Child and Parents." *Behavior Therapy.* In press.

———; Sneed, T. J.; and Foxx, R. M. "Dry Bed Training: Rapid Elimination of Childhood Enuresis." *Behavior Research and Therapy* 12 (1974):147–56.

———, and Thienes, P. M. "Rapid Elimination of Enuresis by Intensive Learning Without a Conditioning Apparatus." *Behavior Therapy* 9 (1978):342–54.

Besalel, V. B.; Azrin, N. H.; and Thienes-Hontos, P. "Evaluation of a Parent's Manual for Training Enuretic Children." *Behavior Therapy.* In press.

Bollard, R. J., and Woodroffe, P. "The Effect of Parent-Administered Dry-Bed Training on Nocturnal Enuresis in Children." *Behavior Research and Therapy* 15 (1977):159–65.

Doleys, D. M.; Ciminero, A. R.; Tollison, J. W.; Williams, C. L.; and Wells, K. C. "Dry-Bed Training and Retention Control Training: A Comparison." *Behavior Therapy* 8 (1977):541–48.

Index

[Page numbers in *italics* indicate illustrations.]

183

184

149

Bringing Up A Brighter, Happier Child

The growth of a child's mind is a wonderful thing to watch.
And it's even more wonderful when you've read up on the
subject. Pocket Books has a fine list of titles about the mental
development of children written by prominent specialists in
the field.

**If you are a parent, or soon plan to be, you'll want these
books for your home library.**

_____	42170	HOW TO RAISE A BRIGHTER CHILD Joan Beck	$2.75
_____	42211	IMPROVING YOUR CHILD'S BEHAVIOR CHEMISTRY Lendon Smith, MD	$2.95
_____	43661	UNDERSTANDING YOUR CHILD FROM BIRTH TO THREE Joseph Church	$2.75
_____	82734	RAISING CHILDREN IN A DIFFICULT TIME	$2.25